Y0-BNX-334

*Southern Living*

# ideas for great
# WALL
# SYSTEMS

*Carved out of an upstairs hallway is a fully equipped computer center with built-in desk and bookcases. Wallspace above the desk is painted with blackboard paint for doodles and messages.*

Oxmoor House®

DESIGN: ALLMILMO SHOWPLACE, A KITCHEN STUDIO

*Colorful system of drawers, cupboards, and cubes can be arranged in different ways. The components are finished in satin acrylic lacquer.*

*Southern Living® Ideas for Great Wall Systems* was adapted from a book by the same title published by Sunset Books.

Book Editor
**Lynne Gilberg**

Research & Text
**Don Vandervort**

Coordinating Editor
**Cornelia Fogle**

Consulting Editor
**Jane Horn**

Editorial Coordinators
**Bradford Kachelhofer, Vicki Weathers**

Design
**Joe di Chiarro**

Illustrations
**Bill Oetinger**

Special Contributors
**Linda Bouchard, Bridget Biscotti Bradley, Barbara Brown, Tishana Peebles, Jean Warboy**

**Cover**
Design: **James Boone, Vasken Guiragossian.** Photography: **Jean Allsopp, Southern Progress Photo Collection.** Architect: **Dave Davis, Dixon Weinstein Architects**

Our appreciation to the staff of *Southern Living* magazine for their contributions to this book.

*Southern Living®* is a federally registered trademark of Southern Living, Inc.

Photographers: **Peter Aaron/Esto,** 27 bottom; **Jean Allsopp,** 6–7, 46 bottom; **American Wood Council,** 12 left; **Lea Babcock:** 56 bottom; **Otto Baitz,** 58 bottom; **Laurie Black,** 15 left, 25 bottom, 35 left, 48, 55 right, 57; **Andrew Bordwin,** 38 top left, 43 bottom, 44 top, 45 bottom; **Peter Christiansen,** 17; **Crandall & Crandall,** 9 right, 25 right, 30, 37 top, 38 bottom, 87 top left, 91 left; **Stephen Cridland,** 4; **Cheryl Dalton,** 9 left, 19, 38 top right, 39, 40 bottom; **Colleen Duffley,** 33, 35 top right and bottom right; **eurodesign, ltd.,** 5 right, 8, 13 left, 43 top, 52, 86 bottom; **Michael E. Garland,** 24, 25 top left, 34, 36 top, 55 left; **Shelley Gazin,** 31; **Jeff Goldberg/Esto,** 10 right; **Philip Harvey,** 2, 28 top, 37 bottom, 42, 44 bottom, 49 top right and left, 50, 56 top, 66, 78, 82, 83, 84, 85, 86 top, 87 top right, 87 bottom left, 87 bottom right, 93 top; **Lexington Furniture Industries,** 69 left; **David Duncan Livingston,** 20; **Renee Lynn,** 41 bottom, 49 bottom right; **Sylvia Martin,** 22, 46 top, 47 bottom, 68, 69 right, back cover bottom; **Norman McGrath,** 12 right, 28 bottom, 45 top, 47 top, 61 top, 63, 64, 93 bottom; **Emily Minton,** 16, 23 bottom, 29 top, 40 top, 60, 90, 91 right, back cover top; **Michael J. Mugridge,** 41 top; **John O'Hagan,** 26, 27 top, 36 bottom, 76; **Cesar Rubo,** 61 bottom; **Rudolph Schmutz,** 72; **Meg McKinney Simle,** 1, 53, 58 top; **Techline by Marshall Erdman and Associates, Inc.,** 11, 73; **Vander-Schuit Studio,** 32, 59; **Don Vandervort,** 29 bottom; **Visador Company,** 13 right, 51; **Darrow M. Watt,** 23 top right; **Wellington Hall, Ltd.,** 10 left; **Russ Widstrand,** 54 bottom; **Wood-Mode, Inc,** 54 top, 74.

## Stow, store, stack, rack, pile, file, and more

Versatile and efficient, today's wall systems can help you solve a myriad of display, storage, and organization problems. But with so many types of systems on the market, choosing the right one is a challenge.

That's where this book can help. It begins with a planning primer to help you identify your storage needs and become familiar with the basic types, styles, and materials of wall systems.

Next, you'll find a colorful collection of wall units that you can use for inspiration as you plan your own. Finally, there's a detailed look at components and accessories to guide you in making informed buying decisions and distinguishing quality materials and workmanship.

For their help, we thank Allmilmo Showplace, A Kitchen Studio; School's Kitchen Tour; El Cerrito Lumber; eurodesign, ltd.; Kitchen and Bath Showroom; Osburn Design; Peninsula ASID/Children's Health Council Designer's Showcase; San Francisco Decorator Showcase; and Techline by Marshall Erdman and Associates, Inc.

We extend special thanks to Fran Feldman for carefully editing the manuscript and to JoAnn Masaoka Van Atta for styling some of the photographs.

10 9 8 7 6 5 4 3 2
First printing January 2000
Copyright © 2000 by Oxmoor House, Inc.
Book Division of Southern Progress Corporation
P.O. Box 2463
Birmingham, Alabama 35201
All rights reserved, including the right of reproduction in whole or in part in any form.

ISBN 0-376-09072-3
Library of Congress Catalog Card Number: 99-65012
Printed in the United States

# CONTENTS

## SPECIAL FEATURES

# GETTING ORGANIZED

Books, magazines, electronic equipment, videotapes, compact discs, collectibles, sports gear—the array of belongings most people manage to accumulate over the years is staggering. Yet few homes provide enough space to stow all these objects in an organized way.

When you can't stack your stereo gear any higher, when your favorite collection is languishing in boxes in the basement, and when you can't wedge one more book onto your shelves, it's time to think about how you can make better use of your present storage space—and how you can add to it without having to remodel your home or move to a new one.

One way to create a workable, lasting solution to your organization and storage needs is to introduce wall systems into your home. Whether you buy components off the shelf or hire a cabinetmaker to custom build units

ARCHITECT: JERRY L. WARD. DESIGN: GREGG LAMOTHE

*Towering wall system beneath a cathedral ceiling takes full advantage of the available space. Because the ladder starts 4 feet above the floor, it doesn't interfere with the storage cabinets below or the broad countertop that serves as a desk as well as a tall first step.*

for you, you can make your home work harder and smarter to calm the chaos of clutter.

What exactly is a wall system? Think of it as a wall-mounted, freestanding, or built-in system of components and accessories that's used for organization, storage, and display. It can go in virtually any room of the house and can be used to store just about any household object.

Despite its name, a wall system need not always stand against a wall or be built into one. Instead, it can project from a wall into a room or even stand alone in an open area.

Of course, deciding that you need some type of wall system is just the beginning. The next step is to evaluate your storage needs: just what objects in your home need to be better organized, where is the best place to put them, and what type of system will work for you? The first chapter of this book will guide you through the preliminaries.

As you begin to narrow down your choices, use the photos that follow for inspiration and ideas. Take note of how and where objects are stored. You'll no doubt discover solutions you never thought of before.

Finally, you'll be ready to focus on the exact storage unit that's right for you. The last chapter will familiarize you with the myriad choices in organization and storage furnishings and accessories on the market today. In no time at all, you'll be enjoying the ease and convenience of a clutter-free environment with a place for everything and everything in its place.

DESIGN: SAM TAYLOR, ASSOCIATED DESIGN

DESIGN: EURODESIGN, LTD.

*Open for business, this home office emerges from high-efficiency cabinetry. When work is done, the printer shelf rides on tracks into the cabinet and a retractable door swings down. The keyboard tucks away and folding doors conceal the monitor.*

*Like a secret passage, bookshelves swing out to reveal a storage cache. Hinged to door jambs, the swinging modules, which ride on heavy-duty casters, offer back-to-back shelving.*

CABINETMAKERS: PHILIP AND DALE ABERCROMBIE

*Filling an entire wall with custom bookshelves gives this living room the air of a library. They look like a permanent installation, but they are freestanding portable units screwed to the wall that can move with the owners.*

# A LOOK AT YOUR OPTIONS

The term "wall system" is actually a catchall phrase referring to a broad category of organization and storage furnishings. Also called wall units or storage systems, wall systems can range from a simple grouping of shelves on a wall to extensive component systems that include cabinets with doors, adjustable shelves, stacks of drawers, a desk, even a drop-down bed.

In fact, wall systems come in a staggering array of variations. You can buy inexpensive pine shelving, fine hardwood cabinetry, a modern laminate component system, a reproduction Shaker wall unit, high-end lacquered cabinetry, and scores of other types. Your options span a wide range of materials, styles, sizes, and finishes.

One feature characteristic of many, but not all, wall systems is modularity. Components and accessories are often sized so they can be interchanged and reconfigured as your needs change—shelves can be raised or lowered, drawers can be refitted, and cabinets can be moved from one location to another. It's this versatility and flexibility that make modular wall systems popular in so many homes today.

## FURNITURE OR BUILT-INS?

Broadly, there are two decidedly different categories of wall systems: furniture pieces and built-ins. Furniture pieces can be either freestanding or designed to attach to a wall for support. Built-ins are custom fitted to specific locations in your home and are usually constructed and installed by a cabinetmaker or other woodworking professional.

The first choice you'll need to make when you're considering a wall unit is whether to buy furniture or construct a built-in. Here's a closer look at the benefits and drawbacks of each.

**Furniture.** An obvious advantage of furniture is that it's movable. If it doesn't work in one location or is no longer needed there, you can move it to another area or room. And it goes along with you when you move. Moreover, you can see exactly what you're

DESIGN: EURODESIGN, LTD.

*Capturing a corner, this modular wall system features a range of components, from conventional cabinets, shelves, and drawers to a specialized corner cabinet, a drop-down desk, display bays, and built-in low-voltage lighting.*

*Cleverly fitted into a recess in the wall, this tall, custom-made cabinet mimics the rough-hewn Trastero-style furniture popular in the South-west. Behind the colorful doors, a television set sits securely on a pullout shelf in a 30-inch-deep bay.*

*Deep, built-in bookshelves frame the doorways of this foyer, turning it into the family library. Carefully detailed woodwork integrates the bookcases into the room.*

getting in the store and can usually, though not always, get quick delivery.

Some types of storage furniture are intended to be fastened to the wall for support. By attaching shelving or storage units to walls or ceilings, you can eliminate the need for shelf backs or other supports, reducing the cost. If the unit doesn't extend to the floor, you also free up the floor space below the unit for another purpose.

One drawback to buying ready-made or ready-to-assemble storage furniture is that you may not always be able to get exactly the size and configuration you want. Though buying components offers a great deal of flexibility, no system can meet every possible need.

**Built-ins.** With a built-in, you can tailor the space precisely to your storage needs. Though premade cabinetry may be installed in a built-in storage unit, built-ins are, for the most part, custom made to your specifications by a cabinetmaker, finish carpenter, or other professional.

Built-ins are particularly well suited to odd-size spaces in your home where a piece of storage furniture can't fit—for example, within a thick wall, under a staircase, over a doorway, and around windows.

When they're built into existing walls, they save valuable floor space.

Perhaps the most favored feature of built-ins is that they can look almost "seamless" in a room. When designed to complement a room's architectural style, they can project a sense of belonging, taking on the look of a highly efficient, integrated storage wall rather than just a bookshelf. Though they don't move with you, built-ins are considered permanent improvements that can return value when you sell your home.

An obvious drawback to built-ins is their expense. Like anything that is custom built, a built-in unit can be very costly, though the price will vary depending on size, materials, and the complexity of the design.

## STYLE & DESIGN

Because of their sheer size, wall systems generally play a dominant role in a room's interior design. They can enliven a room through a mix of texture, visual interest, and color or provide a quiet backdrop through symmetry and simplicity. They can project whimsy, the latest trends, or a sense of deep-rooted tradition.

DESIGN: WELLINGTON HALL, LTD.

*Combining a solid oak ladder and fluted maple detailing with hollow-core birch-veneered uprights, this elegant wall system gains its rich, harmonious appearance from a pickled pine finish applied over all. The ladder support is brass-plated steel.*

*Custom display nooks flank a built-in bed system. Glass shelves rest on solid hardwood supports; a decorative hardwood valance conceals lighting.*

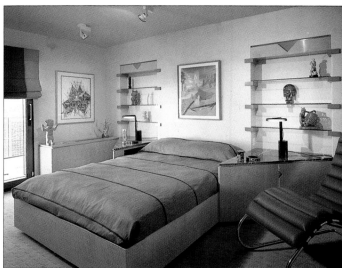

DESIGN: NANCY LAVINE AND RITA MARKS

Whether you buy premade or ready-to-assemble furniture or custom build a unit, you can create a look that matches any decor, style, or personal preference. American country pieces, for example, typically have simple lines with sparse, unpretentious detailing, as befits a style created by people in rural areas using modest, hand-held tools. Contemporary pieces, while also characterized by simple, clean lines, are strong and sophisticated, with form often taking precedence over decoration.

The idea is to select or design a unit that will complement your home's style and furnishings. If you're building your own unit and want a contemporary look, design it with unadorned, simple lines. Ornate moldings and carved door and drawer fronts lend old-world charm.

Color can be used to express style, too. For a sleek, sophisticated appearance, choose black, in either a matte or a shiny finish. Wood tones, from light to dark, are characteristic of a more traditional style, but a unit painted white will also enhance the formal tone of a traditional living room. For a fresh, contemporary look, consider a bright color.

Manufacturers of wall systems offer replicas and reproductions of nearly every decorating style.

# MATERIALS

Most wall systems are made of a veneer of wood or laminate over a core of particleboard or plywood. A very few systems are made of solid wood. Keep in mind that wood and laminates are distinctly different in both their look and their properties. The one you choose will depend on your individual needs and preferences.

**Wood.** Whether the unit is made of solid wood, or wood veneer over particleboard or plywood panels, wood gives a warm, natural look. Solid wood is more durable, more elegant, and, not surprisingly, much more expensive than wood veneer. But wood-veneered panels are less likely to warp and are much more affordable because they require less handwork and utilize wood by-products for the panel interiors.

Woods are classified as either hardwoods or softwoods, terms that refer to the origin of the wood, not its hardness (hardwoods are usually, but not always, harder than softwoods). Hardwoods come from deciduous trees, softwoods from conifers.

Those hardwoods used for furniture make more precise joints, hold fasteners better, and are more resistant to wear than softwoods. Hardwood species favored for furniture include light-toned woods such as oak, ash, beech, birch, and maple and dark-toned species such as cherry, walnut, and mahogany.

Most softwoods are less expensive, easier to tool, and more readily available than hardwoods. Popular softwoods include fir and pine. If you plan to paint or stain the pieces, either of those choices is appropriate.

Wood is given a finish for both protection and appearance. Many different options are available, as explained on page 88.

**Laminate.** Because they're durable, easy to clean, and available in a wide range of colors and patterns, plastic laminates and films are popular surfacing materials for wall systems.

The laminate that covers the particleboard core is applied in one of three ways. The cheapest and least durable method utilizes a vinyl or paper surface film. This film, available in a range of colors and simulated wood grains, is very thin and can peel away from the core panel.

The next grade of product is called melamine, a layer of special paper impregnated with melamine resin. Because it's relatively durable and affordable, this material is quite common. It, too, is sold in many colors and patterns.

Thicker high-pressure laminates are the most durable and costly of the group. These materials come in many colors, patterns, textures, and finishes. Some are appropriate for flat (countertop) surfaces; others are specified only for vertical planes, such as cabinet doors or sides.

DESIGN: TECHLINE BY MARSHALL ERDMAN AND ASSOCIATES, INC.

*Warm oak veneer blends with the high-tech black laminate surfaces of this contemporary modular wall system. The ready-to-assemble cabinetry features heavy-duty imported hardware.*

# DESIGNING A WALL SYSTEM

Even the most elaborate wall system won't be satisfactory if it doesn't provide the right spaces in the right places for the items you need to organize. That's why deciding *where* to put your wall system, as well as *what* to put into it, is so important.

## ROOM-BY-ROOM SOLUTIONS

Look carefully at each room's layout and areas suitable for display and storage. In a room with a fireplace flanked by alcoves, consider taking advantage of those areas for handsome built-in shelving. In a particularly small room, think about running a single bookshelf along a wall, or completely around the room, just above the doorjambs. For a room with multiple elements, how about a continuous wall system that wraps around those elements, drawing them together visually?

**Living areas.** Whether your family congregates in an informal living room, a family room, a den, or a family kitchen, that's the place where such family activities as game playing, reading, watching television, and listening to music occur. Every one of those activities involves paraphernalia. It's easy to understand why such an area seems to attract clutter.

Because they're so versatile, modular wall systems are especially popular in family living areas. Equipped with adjustable shelving, cabinets, drawers, television bays, and other specialty options, these units can organize myriad objects. But virtually any piece of storage furniture or built-in can help contain the clutter.

In more formal living areas, wall systems offer display and storage opportunities. A built-in or ready-made unit that combines open shelving and cabinets can exhibit art objects and prized collections as well as conceal audio equipment and accessories.

**Dining areas.** What's more useful in a dining room than a wall system featuring deep cabinets, drawers, and shelves to hold dishes, glassware, serving pieces, and even tablecloths? When such a unit is combined with a countertop, it also provides a buffet-style serving area.

Where space is at a premium, a dining room that's used only part-time for dining can serve other roles as well. A wall system outfitted with a fold-down desk, file drawers, and cabinets can provide efficient office space that's easily camouflaged when company arrives. Or how about a cabinet filled with

DESIGN: AMERICAN WOOD COUNCIL

*Twin storage and display bays flanking the fireplace contribute to the room's formal symmetry.*

DESIGN: AMY SCOTT

*High-efficiency custom cabinetry finished with crown molding serves both the dining room and adjacent areas.*

audio equipment wired to speakers throughout the house?

If your dining area is part of a large kitchen or an extension of your living room, a wall system, whether it reaches to the ceiling or is just waist high, can effectively divide the space and create the effect of a separate dining room.

**Bedrooms.** In recent years, bedrooms have become much more than just rooms of repose. They often house video and audio gear, fitness equipment, home office areas, library corners, and more.

Because space is limited in most bedrooms, wall systems that store both clothing and other gear are particularly useful. In a bedroom, a large wall unit can stand in for conventional dressers. In children's rooms, units that include low bookshelves, a desk, and drawers encourage neatness.

**Utility areas.** Laundry rooms, workrooms, porches, and other functional areas of a home can utilize shelving and cabinetry to keep tools and supplies organized. Because access is often more important than beauty in those areas, utility shelves and cabinets are often sufficient for general storage.

A safety note: If you have small children, plan to store dangerous items, such as power tools and toxic chemicals and cleansers, on high shelves in locked cabinets.

**Kitchens and bathrooms.** In kitchens and bathrooms, it seems as if there's never enough space for everything. Perhaps you can place a wall unit in a corner or put up some display shelving around a window. Unused kitchen wall space, even an area just a few feet wide, can accommodate a mini-office equipped with shelving for cookbooks, a desktop, and drawers. Under a window or along an unused wall, a wall unit, even one that's not very deep, can expand available display and storage area.

## ITEM-BY-ITEM SOLUTIONS

Only when you know exactly what you want to store, how often you'll need each object, and whether you want the object to be in view or concealed can you design a successful wall unit.

Plan to keep frequently used items readily available: in shallow drawers, on easily reached shelves, or at the front of cabinets. Seldom-used objects can be kept on very low or very high shelves or toward the back of cabinets.

Remember to take into account objects' sizes and shapes and whether your needs are likely to change in the future. Particularly heavy objects demand strong shelves; for information, see pages 78–79.

**Dishes and glasses.** An armoire, hutch, or other freestanding cupboard or cabinet with glass or solid

DESIGN: EURODESIGN, LTD.
INTERIOR DESIGN: LILY T. SACHS

*Modular wall system manages study, hobby, and play gear; as the child grows, modules can be reconfigured.*

DESIGN: VISADOR COMPANY

*Efficient system of rods and slatted hardwood shelving wrings generous storage from a stingy space.*

doors provides plenty of space for china and glassware and also helps keep them dust-free. Built-in units that include drawers, adjustable shelves, and cabinets are also good organizers. Stacks of dishes can be very heavy, so be sure shelves are strong and well supported.

For display, consider a single shelf that runs along a wall at eye level or just above head height, perhaps at the same height as the tops of windows. Interior lighting in china cabinets with glass shelves highlights prized possessions.

If you live in an area prone to earthquakes, opt for a cabinet with doors that can be locked or latched closed.

**Books.** Usually, books are stored on open shelving where they can be easily seen and reached. In general, it's best to place heavy books and reference works on the lower tiers of a shelf system. Art books can go at eye level, and paperbacks can be arranged on higher shelves.

**Magazines.** Unless you recycle them regularly, magazines can quickly overwhelm whatever space you have for them. For easy reference, consider special binders or magazine holders that slide onto shelves like books. Or you can store magazines in flat stacks, ideally behind cabinet doors. Make sure shelves are strong and well supported; stacks of magazines are very heavy.

**Collectibles.** How you display special pieces depends on their need for protection, security, and lighting. A ready-made or built-in unit with glass shelves, sliding glass doors, and interior lighting allows you to enjoy your collection and, at the same time, keep it safe, secure, and clean. Some collectibles can be kept on open shelves; others can be stored in drawers or cabinets.

## Ideal Shelving Dimensions

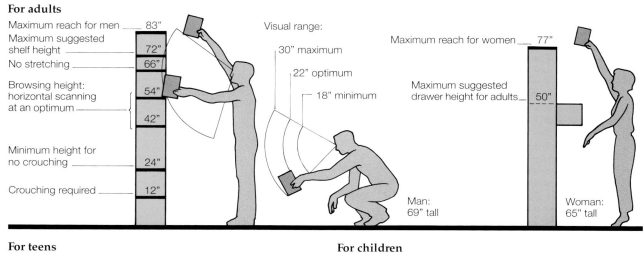

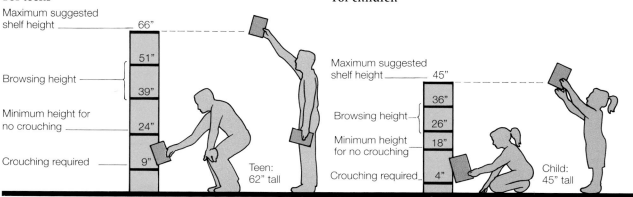

*Well-designed shelving units are sized for easy reach and comfortable browsing. The "right" height for shelves varies depending on the user.*

# Some Typical Sizes of Books, Records, Discs & Tapes

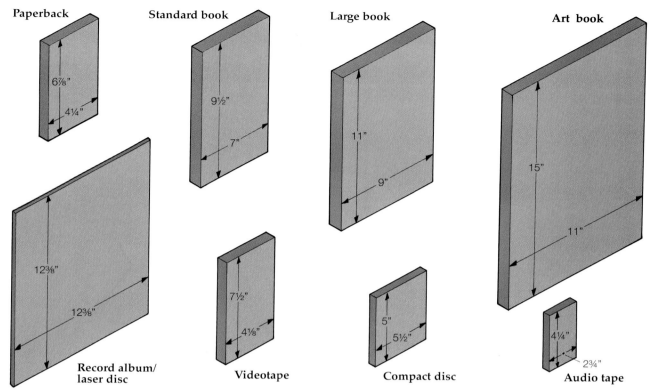

*Here are standard sizes for books, records, and tapes. Adjust shelving to fit the contents, allowing an extra inch or two for easy access.*

**Electronic gear and supplies.** Televisions, stereos, tape decks, compact disc players, and speakers have unique storage requirements. For help organizing electronic equipment, see pages 16–17.

## SIZING YOUR WALL SYSTEM

Whether you're commissioning custom cabinetry or buying a manufactured wall system, knowing the sizes and shapes of the objects you want to organize will help you design or buy an appropriate unit and ensure that those items will fit properly in it.

**Shelf height.** The illustration on the facing page shows norms for fitting shelving to people. While they're not inflexible rules, these are generally accepted standards that you may want to follow when designing your system. Don't place shelves out of reach—note that the recommended height for the highest shelf is 6 feet, unless you have a ladder or stool to help you reach its contents.

**Shelf size.** Though square footage is a good measure of floor space, think in terms of linear footage when figuring your shelving needs. A single shelf 6 feet long offers 6 linear feet of storage. A tall unit with six shelves, each 6 feet long, offers 36 linear feet of storage.

To get a rough idea of the linear footage of shelving you need, simply measure the linear footage of the books, records, and other items you intend to store. Allow extra room for expansion and open display space.

Shelf depth and height depend on the size of the objects you intend to put there. Adjustable shelves have the most flexibility; to determine the right height for fixed shelves, measure the objects that will go there and add an inch or two for head space. The drawing above shows the amount of space some common articles require.

Shelf length depends on the material from which the shelf is made and the weight of the objects that it will support.

DESIGNER: CANDY LLOYD, CANDLER LLOYD INTERIORS, INC.

*Store-bought media cabinet is configured specifically to handle home electronics. An oversize bay surrounds a large-screen television. Related video and audio gear sits behind glass doors.*

The shape, size, lighting, and acoustics of a room will all affect performance. For a true home-theater environment, the room should be at least 10 by 14 feet. Also, take into account any glare from windows that could affect viewing.

Make sure there's sufficient lighting in the area to see titles on records and tapes and for reading equipment controls. If possible, route wires for lighting and electrical hookups behind the unit. If you're building a custom unit, consider including an interior lighting system. Because fluorescent light may cause interference, use incandescent lighting near a tuner or receiver. (For more information on lighting, turn to page 90.)

# EQUIPMENT REQUIREMENTS

Begin by making a list of the components you own and those you may want to add later, and note their measurements. Also count up your accoutrements, such as tapes, compact discs, and accessories. Decide what you'll house in the wall system and what components (speakers, for example) need to be nearby.

**Components.** Positioning electronic components takes careful planning. You'll want them placed conveniently and accessibly, protected from overheating, and situated for optimal performance. For example, a cassette deck needs to be at a height that makes it easy to load and where you can see the tape that's in the machine; a turntable must have sufficient head height so it can be operated, or it must be on a pullout shelf; a television can be viewed most comfortably at seated eye level; and an amplifier, which heats up when it's on, should never be placed directly under another piece of equipment.

Pay strict attention to manufacturer's recommendations, particularly in regard to ventilation. Inadequate ventilation, even in a unit without doors, can ruin your equipment. Though ventilation holes at the back and top of a unit may suffice, you may need to install an exhaust fan if several pieces of equipment are grouped in one section.

When using equipment, leave the doors open to increase air circulation. Make sure that doors on a television cabinet swing open far enough so they don't obstruct your view, or use retractable doors.

If possible, choose a cabinet with a removable back for easy access to equipment. This arrangement also makes routing wires much simpler.

ARCHITECT: BERNARD STEIN

*Custom media cabinet features drawers and pullout shelving for CDs and tapes. Retractable doors open to reveal the television and related gear.*

**Tapes, records, and compact discs.** For small items, such as cassette tapes, drawers offer the most efficient storage. Don't place them much higher than waist level. The best drawers pull out their entire length when opened. If you don't have room for drawers, special organizers available commercially can keep your tapes, compact discs, records, and accessories in order on shelves or in cabinets.

Store videotapes vertically. Place tapes, compact discs, laser discs, and records away from heat sources. Speakers and motorized equipment produce magnetic fields, so keep magnetic tapes at least a foot away from them.

**Speakers.** If your speakers are unshielded, be sure they're located at least 12 inches from the television screen to prevent picture distortion. For a home-theater setup, center the video screen between the front speakers; if your system includes a center speaker, place it directly over or under the screen.

For best audio results, speakers should not be directly centered between the floor and the ceiling and should be at least a foot away from the wall. For optimum stereo separation, speakers need to be at least 5 feet away from each other.

If you intend to put your speakers inside the cabinet, check the manufacturer's directions to be sure they can be used effectively in an enclosure.

# WORKING WITH PROFESSIONALS

Most wall systems rely on experienced professionals for their design and installation. If you're putting in a custom unit, you may want to get design help from an architect, interior designer, or other professional designer. For the actual construction of the unit, you'll rely on a cabinetmaker, woodworker, or furniture maker (or perhaps a contractor if you're involved in a larger project).

Specialists, such as kitchen and bath designers and lighting professionals, can contribute their expertise to a project. For ready-made units, turn to showroom or retail sales professionals familiar with the variety of products on the market.

## HOW PROFESSIONALS CAN HELP

Unless you plan to design, build, and install a wall system yourself, you'll want to enlist the help of others who are expert at their trades. Here's a look at some of the professionals who can help you and guidelines on how to work with them successfully.

**Architects.** Licensed by the state, architects have degrees in architecture and are trained in all facets of building design and construction. An architect can design a built-in system integrated with the room's style and appearance. Some architects may hire an interior designer for storage that falls into the "furnishings" category.

If you're working with an architect on a remodel or a new home, your architect may also design the storage components.

**Interior designers.** For a large wall system that will dominate a room, you may want to consult an interior designer. Interior designers and decorators specialize in decorating and furnishing rooms and can offer fresh, innovative ideas and advice. They also have access to designer showrooms and other resources not available at the retail level (to visit such showrooms, you usually must be accompanied by a credentialed designer or architect). Many designers belong to the American Society of Interior Designers (ASID), a professional organization.

Discuss your designer's fee structure and method of billing. Some designers work on a fee basis; others charge an hourly rate. Still others will add a charge to the furnishings you buy through them. One good arrangement is to work out an hourly rate with a "not-to-exceed" clause.

Related professionals are kitchen and bath designers. These specialists concentrate on specifying fixtures, cabinetry, appliances, and materials for the kitchen and bath. Their talents in cabinet design easily translate to other rooms of the house.

**Lighting designers.** A lighting designer specifies placement of lighting and the fixtures necessary to achieve the level of light required. Such a specialist can help you plan interior or exterior lighting for a media center, a display cabinet or shelving, a home-office wall system, or a similar setup.

**Retail specialists.** Showroom personnel, furniture store salespeople, building center staff, and other retailers can help you choose and, in some cases, combine components to create a wall organizer that's right for you. In fact, this kind of help may be all you need if your requirements are fairly minor. For a larger job, check the specialist's qualifications carefully. Though some salespeople are quite capable and helpful, others may be motivated simply to sell you more goods or a particular line of products.

For design help at the retail level, you generally provide a rough floor plan of the room where you'll be installing storage. If possible, also submit a rough elevation drawing of what you would like. Retailers who sell ready-to-assemble component systems will often provide a finished plan and/or a materials list if you buy the goods from them. Some firms do the work by computer simulation; others draw plans. Most retailers offer installation services.

**Media center specialists.** Just as with custom wall systems, cabinetmakers, architects, and interior designers are your best resources for designing a custom media center. Remember, however, that planning effective housing of audio and video gear is a specialized art. Be sure the designer you select has experience working with electronics or will consult with experts.

Some electronics retailers have qualified professionals who can work with you and your designer on both planning and installation. (For more on storing electronic gear, see pages 16–17.)

**Custom woodcrafters.** A number of different tradespeople, including cabinetmakers, woodworkers, furniture makers, and finish carpenters, build shelves and cabinetry. Though there is some overlap, each of these trades is slightly different. To find these people, look in the Yellow Pages under "Cabinetmakers," "Carpenters," "Furniture—Custom Made," "Kitchen Cabinets," and "Woodworkers."

Nearly all cabinetmakers, whether they're dealers selling manufactured products or local woodshops that build custom cabinets, focus on kitchens and bathrooms. They typically install the units.

Woodworkers offer services similar to those offered by small cabinet shops. The main difference is that they're more likely to handle jobs, such as building furniture, that are outside the realm of normal cabinets.

Custom furniture makers work in their own shops and typically handle difficult—and often expensive—projects.

Finish carpenters are hired by contractors or homeowners to install trimwork and cabinetry in a house. Their talents range from stapling moldings in place to fine cabinetmaking. Most finish carpenters don't have workshops, so the work is typically done on-site, ruling out complex cabinetmaking (though they do install premade cabinets).

**Contractors.** State or local licensing ensures that contractors have met minimum training standards and have a specified level of experience. Licensing does not guarantee that they are good at what they do. Usually, a general contractor will oversee a homebuilding or remodeling project, hiring subcontractors to do the work. In this case, the contractor is responsible for the quality of work and materials and for paying the subcontractors.

# SELECTING A PROFESSIONAL

Whether you're selecting a designer, a cabinet builder, or a contractor, start by getting referrals from people you know who have had similar work done—nothing beats a personal recommendation. Or you can turn to the Yellow Pages for help. Then call several candidates. On the telephone, first ask whether each handles the type of job that you want done and can work within the constraints of

*Colorful custom wall system, a collaborative effort between the homeowner and a professional designer, plays an integral role in this room's interior design.*

your schedule. If so, arrange meetings and ask them to be prepared with references and photos of previous jobs. When choosing a cabinetmaker, you may want to visit former clients to check the professional's work firsthand.

Ask each candidate for a firm bid, based on exactly the same plans or discussions. Have your plans—or intentions—as complete as possible. You don't have to accept the lowest bid; it's more important to choose a reliable, responsible person whose work you admire.

For some jobs, you may want a written contract, which binds and protects both you and the person you hire. Not just a legal document, a contract is also a list of the expectations of both parties. When every detail is written down, a contract can help minimize the possibility of misunderstandings later. Whether the contract is a standard form or one composed by you, look it over carefully before both you and the professional sign it.

The contract should clearly identify the participants and define all work to be done, including specific descriptions of all the materials that will be used in the project, the time schedule, and the payment schedule. It should include a set of working drawings.

DESIGN: SHARON CAMPBELL, ASID

# GREAT WALL SYSTEMS

Need inspiration? This chapter is packed with colorful examples of many different kinds of wall systems, from up-to-the-minute media centers to traditional shelving, all designed to solve specific organization challenges. As you peruse the pages, think about what materials were used and how the design relates to the room. Note also where the units are placed and how particular objects are displayed or stored in them.

Though many of the wall systems shown here were designed for a specific area and purpose, you can adapt them to nearly any situation.

For more information on components, turn to the chapter beginning on page 67.

*Maple cubes on the wall echo the lines of the railing and furnishings in this contemporary great room. The wall system's natural wood finish, analine-dye colored accents, and simple, geometric design produce a fresh, whimsical attitude. Open shelves provide display space; drawers maximize storage.*

# SIMPLY SHELVES

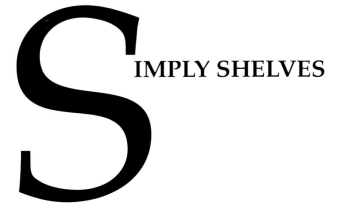

*The floor-to-ceiling built-in shelves behind this open kitchen line hallways and have multiple functions: to add storage, provide display space, and add visual excitement to the home's contemporary interior.*

ARCHITECT: A RUSSELL VERSACI, AIA, VERSACI NEIMANN & PARTNERS

Cubicles of white oak partition a living room and dining area/gallery. On this side, shelves stand about 5 feet high; up the stairs and on the unit's other side, the top, a slab of slate, is at lower buffet height.

To convert a front parlor into a reading room, one full wall was wrapped with bookshelves. As the ceilings in the room are almost 11 feet high, the antique rolling ladder is more than just decorative.

ARCHITECT: SARAH TATE, TATE HILL JACOBS ARCHITECTS

# SIMPLY
## SHELVES

ARCHITECT: ANDY NEUMANN, AIA, SEASIDE UNION ARCHITECTS

*Mounted on wooden brackets to a board-and-batten wall, these simple painted wooden shelves convey a rustic cottage look appropriate for the country-style kitchen. At the bottom, a grouping of narrow shelves, sandwiched between two appliance garages, keeps spices close at hand.*

Shallow shelves neatly accommodate a child's possessions. Though they seem to cantilever from the wall, the shelves are held by lengths of angled steel. The cabinet on the left stands on tall, wrought-iron legs and is fastened to the wall.

DESIGN: CALVIN L. SMITH ASSOCIATES, INC.

Bold and architectural in appearance, these thick shelves are actually laminate-covered plywood boxes. They were mounted to the wall using two-part cabinet mounting clips.

DESIGN: AL DUARTE

Easy and inexpensive, bookshelf boards mounted on adjustable tracks and brackets are a familiar solution to the need for simple display and storage space. The shelves are painted to complement the room.

# BOOK WALLS

Generous two-story library is filled with light and loaded with display and storage space. The hinged bookcase behind the desk (shown at right) is actually the door to the library; when the door is closed, the room becomes a private oasis.

ARCHITECT: ROBERT BELL, AIA

Brimming with books, these built-in bookcases seem as essential to this traditional living room as the walls themselves. The shelves are positioned above wainscoting and fixed in place to preserve their formal look.

Reflective reading seems right at home in this stylish study. The shelving wall was built in sections in a cabinet shop, lacquered, and then installed. The high-gloss, dropped ceiling hides a plug mold fitted with plug-in sockets and reflector bulbs.

ARCHITECT: GIBSON WORSHAM

DESIGN: JOHN F. SALADINO, INC.

# BOOK

## WALLS

When bookshelves scale the walls, as they do in this towerlike study space, a library ladder provides easy access to the upper reaches. The ladder slides along a rail mounted to the shelving. Dynamic architecture and careful detailing infuse distinctive style.

Rich, dark-toned hardwoods and classic design evoke the image of a traditional library. Finely detailed paneling surrounds the books, concealing the wall's support. Brass tubes above the shelves hold miniature lights.

DESIGN: ROBERT W. MILLER, ASID, FLEGEL'S HOME FURNISHINGS

DESIGN: MOORE GROVE HARPER

ARCHITECT: STEPHEN MUSTE. INTERIOR DESIGNER: DENNIS CANNADAY

*Dining rooms are not just for dinner anymore. A wall of floor-to-ceiling bookshelves allows this spacious room to also function as a library and family room.*

# LIBRARY LADDERS

Reaching a book on the top shelf of a bookcase can be a challenge, particularly if the shelf is higher than about 6 feet. To take full advantage of a tall bookshelf, consider extending your reach with the help of a library ladder or step stool.

Several types of folding ladders and step stools are available from office supply stores, furniture dealers, and home improvement retailers. You can also buy movable ladders on locking casters, decorative library stools, and track-mounted library ladders from ladder manufacturers (see pages 94–95).

Track-mounted library ladders, which slide along a horizontal track mounted near the top of a bookshelf, are custom made to fit your bookshelf. One type, a rolling ladder, has rollers at the top and wheels at the base. Another type, a hook-slide ladder, hooks onto the track and can be lifted off and moved to another location. Both are manufactured in different hardwoods, including oak, mahogany, maple, birch, ash, walnut, and cherry, and can be given a variety of different finishes.

DESIGN: JOE RUGGIERO

*Decorative as well as functional, a store-bought faux bamboo ladder leans against a shelf. The lightweight ladder is easy to shuttle from one place to another.*

DESIGN: CALVIN L. SMITH ASSOCIATES, INC.

*Built-in media center, its clear-finished maple doors blending beautifully with the steel-troweled plaster hearth of the fireplace, fits in a corner of this room. Open the retractable doors and voilà!—the electronic equipment appears (shown at left). The thick glass display shelves rest on stainless steel rods.*

# **M**EDIA CENTERS

*Dramatic built-in media center was designed specifically for this electronic gear. Crown molding caps the central television bay. The unit was given a combination of matte black and speckled paint finishes. Short platforms raise the speakers off the floor.*

DESIGN: DRESCO DESIGN

*Flush with the wall, a television and other electronic components tuck into custom-fitted cubbyholes. Ventilation is provided from behind to protect the equipment from overheating. The unit is painted to match the color of the walls.*

DESIGN: ESTELLE LIPSICK ALPERT, FASID, AND RICHARD AINSLIE, ARCHITECT

*With its arched pediment and pickled wood finish, this built-in media cabinet resembles a large armoire. When the doors are opened (see bottom photo), all is revealed—a television and a turntable on pullout shelves, audio equipment stacked above, and record albums neatly arranged in their own cubicles.*

DESIGN: RICHARD MOGAS, AIA

*Perched at the top of a tall cabinet, this television is easy to see from anywhere in the room—it slides out of the cabinet and swivels, and the retractable doors glide out of the way for unobstructed viewing. Below the television, fitted storage organizes a turntable, tapes, and other gear.*

DESIGN: ALLIE CHANG

*Television, speakers, and audio equipment are neatly stored in a column built to reserve wall space for the homeowners' art collection. At the column's base, a drawer is outfitted for tapes. Near the top of the column is a lighted niche for art display.*

ARCHITECTS: OVERLAND PARTNERS, INC.

*Located between the kitchen and the family room, this multipurpose room divider acts as a buffet counter when closed (top photo). Opened, it features drawers sized to hold audio tapes, compact discs, and videocassettes; shelves for audio equipment; and a television cabinet (bottom photo). Two pairs of retractable doors allow complete access and viewing.*

DESIGN: SAM TAYLOR, ASID, ASSOCIATED DESIGN CONSULTANTS

ARTIST: ALICE FELLOWS

Each cubby in this rhythmic staggered shelf system holds a story-telling vignette or tableau. Shown here is a small section of two complete display walls of rural collectibles and the artist's own works.

Punched through a partition wall, square holes strikingly display a twentieth-century glass and pottery collection. Recessed fixtures illuminate the artwork from above. The glass block platforms match the blocks used throughout this contemporary interior.

ARCHITECTS: ROBERT HAMMOND, AIA, AND JAY HUYETT, AIA

# COLLECTION DISPLAYS

*Pueblo-shaped pockets recessed in a plaster wall exhibit a collection of indigenous artifacts that look right at home in this Southwestern-style setting. Miniature low-voltage spots, built into the wall, throw dramatic beams down into each cavity.*

*Bold green wall system displays a majolica collection. Dowels hold platters in place; pitchers queue up along the reveal at the top. Behind glass-paneled swinging doors, a bubble-gum pink china cabinet houses the rest of the collection.*

DESIGN: CALVIN L. SMITH ASSOCIATES, INC.

DESIGN: CARLENE ANDERSON KITCHEN DESIGN, INC.

# COLLECTION

## DISPLAYS

ARCHITECT: MARCH HALL, MMH HALL, ARCHITECTS/PLANNERS, INC.

*Supplementing a small kitchen, this colorful wall unit provides storage, houses a small refrigerator and freezer, offers counter space, and displays interesting ceramics. The shelves, grooved to hold propped plates, are made of birch plywood with maple edging.*

*Extensive collection of cameras, photographs, and photographic memorabilia is revealed in this remodeled attic. The walls and display surfaces are clad in clear-finished yellow pine; the shelving cases have the distinctive grain and grooving of beadboard paneling.*

*Wrapping a doorway, custom-made cabinets show off an impressive array of masks and ceramics. The tall, narrow case on the right takes advantage of a small space. Glass shelves maximize light. Matching units back up to these cabinets on the other side of pocket doors.*

DESIGN: MARK WEBBER, TRADEMARKS

DESIGN: DAVID ASHWORTH AND TOM McNEMAR

# THE ART OF DISPLAY

**B**ookshelves are the perfect vehicle, of course, for storing books. But a wall of solid books can rob a room of interest, visual texture, and decorative focal points. That's why it's important to break up the monotony with objects that are particularly worthy of display.

Gather together the items you want to display, trying to group objects that have something in common, such as color, form, or function. Be selective; you'll be drawing attention to this display, so you don't want it to appear cluttered.

If shelves are adjustable, position them so they align in an attractive, organized way or form an interesting pattern (keep in mind the heights of the objects as you're moving shelves around). It's often effective to create two or three strong horizontal lines that run the length of a wall unit. Placing cabinets and taller spaces near the floor anchors a bay of shelves. You can remove a shelf or two to create a "window" for large objects.

If you need to devote a lot of shelf space to books, avoid placing them wall-to-wall. Instead, shorten the rows, propping the books with bookends, and display art objects or other items in the remaining space.

Don't be hesitant to change your arrangement or move things around once in a while. Shelving should be an active stage for your interests.

*Horizontally stacked books, a sprinkling of artwork, family photographs, repetitive color, and carefully chosen decorative accents combine to produce an eye-pleasing arrangement.*

ARCHITECT: RICK ARCHER, OVERLAND PARTNERS. DESIGNER: ELIZABETH ROBERTS, ADANA AGEE DESIGN ASSOCIATES

*The built-in shelves that flank the fireplace have a stylized design that is true to the Craftsman style of this Houston bungalow.*

*A pair of rounded, natural-wood bookcases flanks a vintage, stacked-stone fireplace. Their shape allows for enough depth in the middle to hold full-size books; at the ends, the bookcases fit flush with the fireplace.*

ARCHITECT: MARK KOHLER, AIA

# FIRESIDE COMPANIONS

DESIGN: AMERICAN WOOD COUNCIL

*Vivid color and strong form call attention to the fireplace wall in this comfortable sitting room. Twin alcoves on either side of the fireplace are highlighted by gracefully arching tops and yellow interiors.*

*Central fireplace is surrounded by a low shelving system that's wired for stereo equipment. The painted shelves blend with the fireplace façade, walls, and other cabinets. The middle shelves are adjustable.*

ARCHITECTS: WILLIAM TURNBULL ASSOCIATES

# CABINETRY FOR KIDS

DESIGN: EURODESIGN, LTD.

Modular wall system offers plenty of flexibility and storage in this child's room. Most of the system is low, within easy reach for a child, including the underbed drawers. Cabinets stow toys; drawers hold clothing. The open shelves are reserved for books and favorite toys. The desktop provides generous work space for homework and hobbies.

Built with the house, this laminate wall system blends nearly seamlessly into the room. Speakers are hidden behind modules covered with speaker cloth; ventilation for the electronic equipment is provided from behind. The built-out section accommodates the room's heating and air-conditioning equipment.

DESIGN: NOEL JEFFREY INC.

Old shelving was enclosed and matching cabinetry and drawers were added to give this nursery a sense of deeply rooted tradition. The vertical closets hold clothing; the drawers and cupboards contain clothes and toys. The patina finish is actually a series of glazed and hand-rubbed layers of blue, purple, and lapis paint. The countertop is a checkerboard of yellow and white tile.

## CABINETRY

## FOR KIDS

*Neat and tidy, this child's room offers abundant storage in drawers beneath the built-in desk and vanity. Natural light from the windows floods the desk; adjustable shelves provide plenty of room for display.*

*Built into an alcove, this loft bed is actually half of an inverted Victorian four-poster. Beneath the bed, modular cabinetry offers generous shelving space. Hinged lids on the base cabinets lift for convenient access; closed, they form a seating ledge.*

DESIGN: ALEXANDER & BYRD, INTERIOR DESIGN ASSOCIATES

DESIGN: LANGSAM RUBIN INTERIORS

DESIGN: BOSTON & WINTHROP

*Geometric shapes and bright colors add to the playfulness of a small child's room. The large modules, covered with durable plastic laminate, provide both closed storage space and open display. Units at the bottom garage small vehicles.*

*Built-in shelves and cabinets seem as much a part of this young girl's room as the walls themselves. The stippled paint finish and gently arching shapes of the wall system accentuate the room's highly decorative feel.*

GREAT WALL SYSTEMS **45**

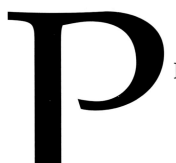

# PRACTICAL PARTITIONS

ARCHITECT: ALAN DYNERMAN

*A furniture-style cabinet painted in bright, folk-art colors divides the space between cozy kitchen and soaring living room. The plain cabinet has a rustic appeal perfectly in keeping with the mood of this farmhouse-style weekend retreat.*

*Dividing the living room from a small playroom is one full storage wall paneled in warm cypress, with shelves on both sides. Children's books are conveniently tucked along the bottom two shelves, while breakable objects warrant higher placement.*

ARCHITECT: CLEMENS BRUNS SCHAUB

Two-sided storage wall separates the kitchen from the sitting area. Open shelves in the corner take advantage of "dead space" created where counters and cabinets intersect in the kitchen. Doors open to shallow cabinets that meet kitchen-side cabinets back-to-back.

DESIGN: AMY SCOTT

Separating kitchen workspace from the dining room is an attractive serving counter with display shelves that make this partition a focal point. Painting the shelves the same shade as the kitchen cabinets ties the spaces together.

# NOVEL SITUATIONS

DESIGN: LINDSTROM CO. AND JC PENNEY

*For watching soaps in the suds, this television is built into a bathroom wall. Above, cubbies hold electronic gear. Ventilation is provided from behind.*

DESIGN: MARY C. PECK, ASID

*A connoisseur's delight, this specialty storage system combines efficient racks for an extensive wine collection with a built-in panel fitted for audio gear.*

ARCHITECT: KENZO HANDA

*Shaped like a traditional Japanese tansu, this boldly geometric niche tucked under the stairs sets a dramatic stage for display.*

*Bookshelf or ladder? The shelving unit that's part of this storage wall is designed to double as a ladder for access to the sleeping loft. Miniature shelves in the corner reclaim unused space for display.*

# **H**ARDWORKING SYSTEMS

DESIGN: VISADOR COMPANY

*Efficient closet system stretches the capacity of this space. Easy-to-install slatted shelves, rods, and supports are made of hardwood and given a golden oak finish.*

*Custom kitchen work center surrounds a cheery window. Tambour doors, like those found on appliance garages, hide office supplies on the left, cooking ingredients on the right. Low-profile, low-voltage lights are fitted into the underside of the hollow shelf above the window.*

*An entire multifunctional room is contained within the confines of this extensive wall system with its array of specialized components and accessories. Included is a fold-down bed, a nightstand, shelving, lighting, a mirror, drawers, space for audio and video gear, and a home office that includes a large pull-down desk.*

DESIGN: EURODESIGN, LTD.

Constructed of laminated birch plywood and trimmed in oak, this custom back door built-in keeps life organized for a busy family of five. Note the lower lip at the bottom of the "lockers" to keep balls from rolling out. Behind cabinet doors, a pull-out drawer holds a large sack of dog food.

DESIGN: PAT CROGHAN, HEINE & CROGHAN ARCHITECTS

## HARDWORKING
## SYSTEMS

*Space-efficient hutch in the dining room is built of custom pine cabinets produced by a large manufacturer. Pullouts, drawers, glass shelves, and other features add flexibility.*

*Home office is both efficient and beautiful, thanks to a custom-built maple wall system. Cubbyholes keep desk supplies within easy reach; glass shelves offer display space.*

DESIGN: WOOD-MODE, INC

DESIGN: CITY CABINETMAKERS

*Utilitarian wall system helps ease a variety of household tasks, among them ironing and laundry. The ironing board folds down from the laminate cabinetry.*

*Tucked into a corner of the breakfast area, this small office provides cookbook storage, a phone center, a bulletin board, and a place to pay bills. The shelves and desk were built during a remodel and painted to match the kitchen.*

DESIGN: WILSONART

GREAT WALL SYSTEMS **55**

# COZY QUARTERS

DESIGN: MIKE MOORE FOR MIKE FURNITURE

DESIGN: AMERICAN WOOD COUNCIL

*Bench seating lines this alcove designed for art display, book storage, and reading. The wall system and benches are made of maple, finished naturally. Doors conceal storage space. The shallow wood counter extends behind the benches for even more display area.*

*Combining a cheerful captain's bed with shelves at the head and foot, this built-in sleeping nook makes a snug nest for a child at bedtime.*

*This comfortable niche flooded with natural light invites reading. Tall shelves on either side put books close at hand.*

ARCHITECTS: SUSAN WITTENBERG, GORDON WITTENBERG, MARK OBERHOLZER, WITTENBERG PARTNERSHIP

The first floor of this Houston house is an open plan, with living area at one end and dining and kitchen at the other. To serve this multi-function space, built-ins stretch along one long wall, functioning in the dining area as bar, office, china cabinet, and pantry.

Matching wall units frame French doors beneath a sweeping ceiling arch. Recessed lighting, set into the soffit, highlights books and art objects.

ARCHITECTS: KEHRT SHATKEN SHARON

# ARCHITECTURAL STATEMENTS

*Honeycomb of fixed shelves is a graphic, Bauhaus-style backdrop in this reading corner. The shelving is custom built from melamine-laminated plywood with oak edge banding. Though the walls aren't perpendicular, the tapered depths of the shelves draw them to a 90° angle.*

ARCHITECTS: RALPH J. ROESLING, AIA, AND MUN YIN KUNG

*Glass doors with gently arched tops
distinguish this version of a
breakfront-style built-in from the
other cabinets in the kitchen. It was
designed to lend the eating area a
little formality, much like a hutch
would in a dining room.*

ARCHITECT: CHARLES AQUINO

ARCHITECT: CHARLES A. PLATT, AIA

*Sweeping bow window is traced by low, hardwood shelving, ideal for book storage. Custom made during construction, this bookcase uses a single, fixed center shelf to maintain visual simplicity.*

*Clear-stained maple cabinets in a highly sculptural form supplement storage in this contemporary kitchen. Simple glass shelves offer elegant display. Low-voltage recessed lighting emphasizes the cabinet's form and illuminates the display.*

ARCHITECT: CHARLES DEBBAS

# CHARACTER, COLOR & DETAIL

*Brightly colored walls, ornate moldings, elliptical arches, and effective lighting combine to give this pair of built-in book-storage niches bold style. The bookcases were added during a remodel.*

*Curling cutouts and gently arched bays that follow the ceiling line offer unique detailing in this straightforward shelving system. The custom-built bookshelves are made of wood. Lights above each bay spotlight art objects.*

# CHARACTER,

## COLOR & DETAIL

*A veneer of anegre, a light-toned African hardwood, combines with solid maple molding in this stunning wall system. Audio and video gear stacks in a corner column; a television hides behind the doors of the protruding cabinet.*

*Cross-hatched cabinet door detailing and doubled verticals above lend texture and visual interest to this highly functional unit.*

DESIGN: DONNA LASSITER/MARK SADLER

ARCHITECTS: CHAPMAN & BIBER

# MAGIC WITH MOLDINGS

Installing decorative moldings adds distinctive style to a custom wall system. Even a standard shelving unit can be dressed up with the addition of moldings. Whether you apply them to the face of the unit or to the surrounding wall, moldings can add classic detailing and visually integrate the wall system into the room.

You can use moldings to create virtually any style, from colonial to postmodern. They come in a wide range of standard profiles, including crown molding, baseboard, and window and door casing. You can also buy reproductions of architectural details, such as pediments, mantels, and pilasters. Before you shop, collect ideas by studying how moldings have been used in the wall systems shown in this book. Then browse through a molding dealer's selection; there you can also see how different moldings can be combined to form interesting profiles.

Moldings are purchased through lumberyards and molding and millwork shops (see page 95). They're priced by the linear foot; in general, they run from about 15 cents per foot for small, simple patterns to more than $15 per foot for ornate architectural styles. Paint-grade pine moldings, which have visible "finger joints" along their length, are much less expensive than oak and other hardwood moldings that can be stained or finished naturally.

Though some restoration-quality architectural moldings are still milled from hardwoods, most ornate moldings are made of polyurethane and are meant to be painted.

If you're having a cabinetmaker or finish carpenter build cabinetry for you, that person will, no doubt, install the moldings, too. But if you're able to handle a miter box and handsaw, you can install moldings yourself. Doing so is a relatively easy, rewarding job.

Before installation, decide whether the moldings will be painted or stained. If you plan to stain them, apply the stain before installation; don't use fillers that might show through the finish. If you're painting the moldings, prime them before installation and add the final paint later.

DESIGN: SUSAN LONG AND GLENDA KNIGHT

*Peaked pediment, custom built from architectural moldings, transforms a simple wall of shelving into a traditional classic. The dark, contrasting walls give the white-painted pediment and shelving special prominence.*

# A SHOPPER'S GUIDE

Y ou've been inspired. You know exactly the type of unit you need to organize your video gear, and you have a wonderful picture—in your mind—of a tall room divider for your living room/dining room area. How do you turn those dreams into reality?

On the following pages, you'll find valuable information on how to shop for ready-made or ready-to-assemble wall systems. Let the details about cabinetry, drawers, shelves and supports, hardware, and lighting guide your choices of appropriate components. Even if you're having the units custom built or you're planning to build them yourself, you'll learn much that will help you make design decisions.

For help in locating many of the products, turn to pages 94–95 for a listing of information sources.

*Doors, drawers, shelves, hardware, lighting—these components and more combine to form successful wall systems. The wood-veneered unit shown here is referred to as semicustom, meaning that standardized parts are arranged and, in some cases, modified to form a custom storage solution.*

# STORAGE FURNITURE

A visit to a retail furniture showroom will unveil a surprising range of ready-made storage and display furnishings. You'll discover state-of-the-art European wall systems, Shaker-style media centers, French étagères, and many styles of curios, chests, and cabinets that can be used individually or in groupings to meet your organization and storage needs.

Buying ready-made storage furniture is usually the quickest and easiest way to solve a storage dilemma. As a rule, storage furnishings are available on short notice. Some stores carry stock, enabling you to take your purchase home the same day. With others, you place an order based on a floor model or catalog and wait a few days or weeks for delivery. Of course, if you choose an imported model that's not stocked domestically, you may have to wait months.

Remember, too, that when you buy ready-made furniture, you can usually see exactly what you're getting in terms of workmanship and quality of materials.

DESIGNER: LEE STOUGH, EWALD ASSOCIATES

*Forget bedroom sets. A light pine armoire provides needed clothing storage and handsome contrast to the black-painted pencil post bed. Rustic baskets divide up the shelves and keep order.*

## Furniture Collections

Many large furniture manufacturers offer collections of furniture, that is, a large number—often as many as 20 or so pieces—of furnishings designed to coordinate in style and finish. Most collections include specialized pieces such as media centers, china cabinets, and storage units.

Some storage furnishings come as a single piece, such as the tall armoire. Others consist of cabinets or units that you can stack up or join side by side. Perhaps the oldest example of the stacked type is the lowboy with a highboy deck. Another example of stacking is the china deck that sits on top of a credenza.

Side-by-side groupings generally include different types of tall cabinets. For example, you can buy a tall curio cabinet as a center piece, add matching pier cabinets on either side of it, and finish off the ends with angled corner units. The result is a coordinated wall of cabinetry suited to a variety of purposes.

A variation of this idea is the European-style modular component system, which is discussed in more detail on page 72.

## Buying Storage Furniture

As with any furniture, quality is often self-evident in the appearance and materials of a product. The best pieces are made of durable, high-grade materials; the quality of the piece is generally reflected in the joinery and detailing of drawers, doors, and similar parts. Of course, the higher the quality, the higher the price.

Fortunately, most showrooms stock lines of furniture from different manufacturers. Shop carefully; you're sure to find furnishings that meet both your needs and your budget.

DESIGN: LEXINGTON FURNITURE INDUSTRIES

DESIGNER: LANDY GARDNER

*An antique corner cabinet combines open and closed shelving and serves as a practical, yet pretty storage piece. The upper display area shows off collectibles, while doors below hide dinnerware and linens.*

*Hand-painted panels decorate the doors of a freestanding media cabinet. The distinctive finish is but one of the many options available in today's reproduction furniture offerings.*

WILKINSON LIBRARY
TELLURIDE, CO 81435

## FURNITURE

You can buy storage furniture at many outlets, including furniture stores, department stores, and designer showrooms. Some furnishings are sold through mail-order catalogs. For complete media centers or furniture to organize electronic gear, visit quality home electronics stores. And if you look around a bit, you can find ready-made storage solutions in many other places, among them antique stores, unfinished furniture stores, and office supply outlets.

As a rule, furniture stores excel in service. Many offer design help, financing, and, if needed, assembly. Most department stores sell from floor models or catalogs. They offer the same services as furniture stores, but, because floor space is limited, you may not find as large a selection. Department stores buy mostly from large, established manufacturers.

Designer showrooms sell ready-made and custom storage furniture and wall systems at wholesale to the design trade (interior designers and architects). To view products in designer showrooms and to make purchases, you must usually be accompanied by a professional designer.

High-end imported modular units are sold through designer showrooms and retail specialty stores, where personnel are trained to create effective designs using the components.

## A Collection of Storage Furniture

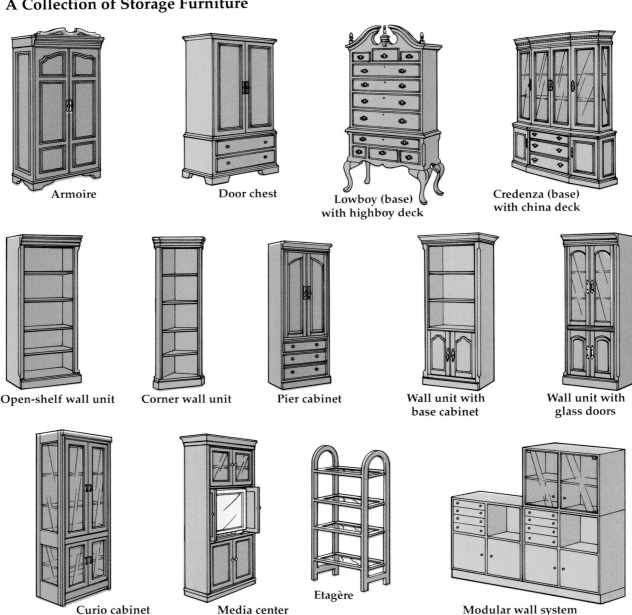

Armoire

Door chest

Lowboy (base)
with highboy deck

Credenza (base)
with china deck

Open-shelf wall unit

Corner wall unit

Pier cabinet

Wall unit with
base cabinet

Wall unit with
glass doors

Curio cabinet

Media center

Etagère

Modular wall system

# ATTACHING TO WALLS & CEILINGS

House walls and ceilings play an important support-ing role in the installation of shelves, cabinets, and wall systems. Whether you're fastening lightweight shelves to a wall, securing a standing unit, or mounting wall cabinets, screwing into wall studs or ceiling joists is the simplest, most secure method of attaching them. If anchor-ing into the house framing isn't prac-tical or your walls are made of ma-sonry, you'll need special fasteners.

## Securing to Studs & Joists

Most house walls and ceilings are not solid; rather, they're made from thin materials—gypsum wallboard, plas-ter and lath, or wood paneling—laid over a framework of studs and joists (see drawing below). Studs, usually 2 by 4 or 2 by 6 lumber, are structural members that run between a sole plate at the floor and a top plate at the ceil-ing. Joists frame the ceiling or upper-story floor.

**Finding studs and joists.** Studs and joists are spaced at regular intervals, usually 16 or 24 inches on center. Once you've found one stud, locating the rest should be easy.

One way to find the first stud is to knock firmly on the wall with the heel of your clenched fist. A solid sound means a stud is behind; a hollow sound tells you to keep knocking.

Another method is to look care-fully at your wallboard or paneling; it often shows where nails have been driven into studs. If nails don't show, use a stud finder, an inexpensive de-vice with a magnetized needle that dances as it nears a metal nail head.

If you're still uncertain, use a small bit to drill exploratory holes in a likely but inconspicuous spot. You'll know when you hit a stud.

The same methods apply to find-ing joists. If you're working on the top (or only) story of a house, you may be able to crawl into the attic and see the placement of the joists.

Once you've found studs or joists, make light marks on the wall or ceiling at the spots where you intend to place fasteners.

**Attaching to studs and joists.** The easiest screws to use on studs and joists are drywall screws, which, when power driven, do not require the drill-ing of a pilot hole. For firm fastening, screws should penetrate the framing member for two-thirds their length.

## Using Special Fasteners

For hanging lightweight shelving where you can't secure it to studs, choose either spreading anchors or toggle bolts (shown below). If you're attaching cabinetry or shelving to ma-sonry walls, use masonry anchors.

**Using spreading anchors.** A spread-ing anchor consists of a bolt and metal sleeve. To use one, you first tap the anchor into a predrilled hole. Then you tighten the bolt, which expands the sleeve against the wall's back side. Finally, you back out the bolt, slip it through the object to be attached, and retighten the bolt in the sleeve.

**Fastening with toggle bolts.** Toggle bolts have spring-loaded, winglike toggles that expand once they're through the wall. Begin by drilling a hole large enough for the compressed toggles. Pass the bolt through the ob-ject to be mounted and screw into the toggles; then slide the toggles through the hole—they'll open on the other side and pull up against the back of the wall when you tighten the bolt.

**Attaching with masonry anchors.** The two main types of masonry an-chors are expanding anchors and lead shields. Both can hold plenty of weight, but the expanding anchor is more re-liable; it features a threaded stud with expanding rings or prongs that grip masonry firmly when a nut is driven home on the stud. Lead shields are hollow-core, threaded sleeves that re-ceive woodscrews or lag screws.

For either type, you use a ma-sonry bit to drill a hole the diameter of the anchor or sleeve and slightly longer; then you gently tap in the de-vice (start a nut on the threads of an expanding anchor to protect them). With an expanding anchor, you slip the object onto the threaded stud and add a washer and nut. With a lead shield, you slip a screw through the object to be attached and drive the screw into the sleeve.

## Hidden Studs & Joists

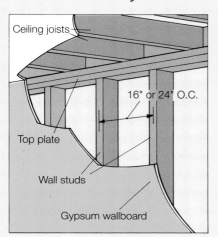

Ceiling joists

16" or 24" O.C.

Top plate

Wall studs

Gypsum wallboard

## Special Fasteners

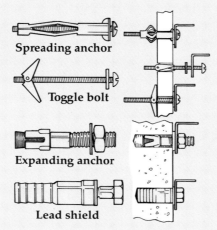

Spreading anchor

Toggle bolt

Expanding anchor

Lead shield

# MODULAR WALL SYSTEMS

Born in Scandinavia, modular wall systems have over the years come to be accepted worldwide as sensible, practical, and beautiful display and storage units. Today, manufacturers offer myriad types, styles, and designs.

## How Modular Units Work

It's easy to understand the appeal of a modular system. The keys to its success are modular design, functional flexibility, and ease of installation. You can combine shelves, cabinets, drawers, and other components to fit your exact needs and space requirements; and, when you move, you can often pack up the pieces and take them with you—and then rearrange them for your new situation.

Most large manufacturers offer scores of components, accessories, and finishes. One manufacturer alone produces more than 200 different components and accessories in three kinds of wood and more than two dozen finishes, with seven kinds of hardware. At the very least, nearly all systems are sold in a range of heights, widths, and depths.

Components often include several types of cabinets, a variety of shelves, several different doors, desk units, drawers, even fold-up beds. In addition, many systems offer a range of special accessories, such as record racks, swiveling pullout television shelves, wine racks, and other helpful organizers. (For more about these special components and accessories, see page 86.)

Despite this staggering diversity, practically all systems allow you to combine differing components and accessories into one integrated unit, enabling you to create a virtually "custom" piece of furniture at stock prices. One way many manufacturers do this is by configuring their components on a 32-millimeter grid, meaning that side panels are drilled every 32 millimeters to receive hinges, shelf pegs, drawer slides, fasteners, and other hardware.

## Preassembled or Ready-to-Assemble?

Some modular systems are largely preassembled; all you need to do is mount the components on supports. With others, you may need to install door fronts on cabinets; still others require that you assemble everything, even the drawers.

This last type, units that come completely disassembled and packed flat in boxes, is referred to as ready-to-assemble, or RTA. Manufacturers of such systems avoid assembly labor costs and high shipping expenses, passing the savings along to you in

*A striking column of drawers climbs the front of this imported, black-lacquered wall system. The tall cabinets hold dishes and tableware conveniently close to where they're used.*

DESIGN: INTERLÜBKE

exchange for a few hours of your time. Other advantages include easy replacement of damaged parts and reduced shipping damage.

Most RTA storage systems are made of melamine, plastic-laminate, or wood-veneered panels that are connected with special knockdown hardware. Assembly is usually a simple job, requiring a few basic hand tools, sometimes included in the package. (Below are instructions for putting together a typical RTA system.)

Remember, however, that modules can be extremely heavy when they're fully assembled; you may need a helper or two. Also, some finished units are so large that they will need to be constructed on-site, in the room where they'll be located.

DESIGN: TECHLINE BY MARSHALL ERDMAN AND ASSOCIATES, INC.

*Ready-to-assemble unit in black laminate features two glass-door cabinets. The television sits on a pullout shelf in a cabinet with retractable doors.*

# BUILDING A READY-TO-ASSEMBLE SYSTEM

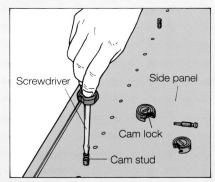

**1. Drive cam studs into holes in side panels until fully seated.**

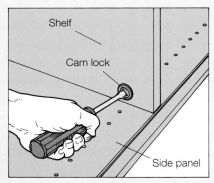

**2. On one side, push shelves onto cam studs; lock in place.**

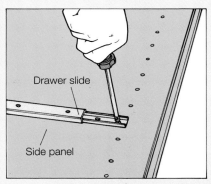

**3. Screw drawer slides to both sides of cabinet. Add second side.**

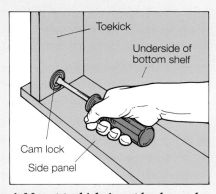

**4. Mount toekick; insert back panel into grooves and screw in place.**

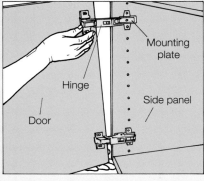

**5. Screw hinges to doors and then to mounting plates on cabinet sides.**

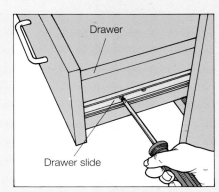

**6. Assemble drawers with glue and dowel pegs; screw to slides.**

# M ANUFACTURED CABINETS

Factory-made cabinets, the type typically used in kitchens and bathrooms, are an important option to consider when you're planning permanent, built-in storage for any room in your house.

Sold through kitchen cabinet dealers, manufactured cabinets come in many styles, from relatively inexpensive stock models to high-end custom creations. You can use them to create storage walls, buffets, home offices, and much more.

If you possess modest carpentry skills, you may be able to install the cabinets yourself (instructions for installing base and wall cabinets appear on page 77). Otherwise, you'll want to call in a professional.

## Traditional or European-style?

On traditional American cabinets, a face frame is added to the front of the cabinet. European-style cabinets are frameless. (Both styles are shown at the top of the facing page.) As a rule, manufacturers specialize in one style or the other, though some make both.

**Face-frame cabinets.** On traditional face-frame cabinets, the raw front edges of each box are masked with a 1 by 2 face frame. Doors and drawers fit in one of three ways: flush; partially inset, with a lip; or completely overlaying the frame.

Because the frame covers all the edges, thin or low-quality panels can be used for the sides, which lowers the price. But the frame takes up space; it reduces the size of the openings, so drawers and slide-out accessories must be significantly smaller than the cabinet's width. Also, hinges for face-frame cabinets are usually visible from the front.

**European-style frameless cabinets.** On frameless cabinets, the raw front edges of the basic box are banded with narrow trim strips. All hardware for doors, drawers, and accessories mounts directly to the panels. Overlay doors and drawer fronts usually fit to within ¼ inch of each other, revealing a thin sliver of the edge trim. Interior components, such as drawers, can be sized almost to the full interior dimensions of the box.

Frameless cabinets usually have a separate toekick pedestal at the base, which allows you to specify a toekick height that's to your liking or to stack base units.

Thanks to absolute standardization of every component, frameless cabinets are unsurpassed in versatility. Precise lines of holes are drilled on the inside faces. These holes are gen-

*Factory-made cabinets scale the wall and run beneath the garden window seat. Built to the specifications of a particular order but based on standard sizes, the unit is typical of manufactured custom cabinets.*

DESIGN: BONNIE SCOTT ARMSTRONG, ASID ASSOCIATE
PRODUCT DESIGN: WOOD-MODE, INC.

erally in the same places, no matter what cabinets you buy, and components just plug right into them.

The basic matrix of all these cabinets is 32 millimeters (32 mm); all the holes, hinge fittings, cabinet joints, and mounts are set 32 millimeters apart.

## Stock, Custom, or Semicustom?

Cabinets are manufactured and sold three different ways: stock, custom, and semicustom. The type you choose will affect the cost, overall appearance, and quality of your storage system. As a rule, custom and semicustom cabinets will be made of better materials—and will look better—than stock.

A sampling of factory-made cabinetry is shown at right.

**Stock cabinets.** Buy cabinets "off the shelf" and save—if you're careful. Mass-produced, standard-size cabinets are the least expensive option; they can be an excellent choice if you clearly understand the cabinetry you need and can work with standard sizes. They're available on short notice.

Manufacturers offer an extensive range of standard sizes. Cabinets are typically made 9 to 48 inches wide, in 3-inch increments.

Base cabinets, 34½ inches tall and 24 inches deep, are made to fit under counters, so they may not have a top panel. Wall cabinets measure 12, 18, 24, 30, 48, or 60 inches high and 12 inches deep.

Tall cabinets—often one of the best components for general storage needs—come 84, 90, and 96 inches tall. Wardrobe, bookcase, and hutch-style cabinets vary from 30 to 96 inches high and from 18 to 24 inches deep.

You can specify door styles and direction of swing, as well as whether side panels are finished. In addition, you can buy trim panels that are cut on-site for filling gaps between cabinetry and walls.

Some stock lines are heavily discounted at some home centers. But buying such cabinets can be a lot like

## Face-frame & Frameless Cabinets

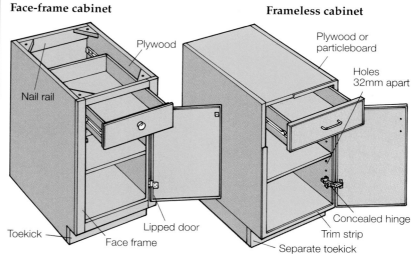

*Thin wood frame covers raw edges of face-frame cabinet (left) and lends rigidity; frameless cabinet (right) is essentially a sturdy box.*

## Typical Manufactured Cabinets

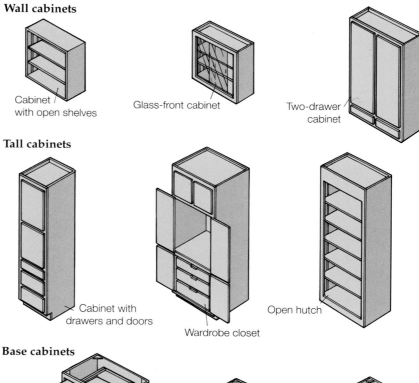

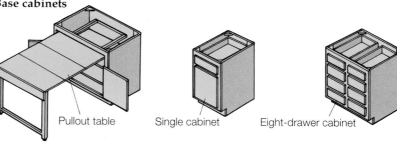

doing your own taxes—no one really volunteers much information that will save you money or clarify your options. If you make a mistake or get bad advice, you're the one who's liable.

**Custom cabinets.** Though some custom cabinets are made by local cabinet shops, most are built by large cabinet manufacturers.

Custom manufacturers make a vast range of standard sizes and finishes, which enables them to use production economies. Standard practice, though, is to alter sizes, finishes, and configurations to meet the specifications of each order as it's received. Such jobs generally cost considerably more than medium-line stock cabinetry and typically take 8 or more weeks for delivery.

**Semicustom cabinets.** Between stock and custom is semicustom cabinetry, or custom systems. An industry hybrid, semicustom cabinets offer the best of both worlds. They're manufactured after an order is placed but take advantage of assembly-line building and standardization of sizes. In essence, these cabinets are middle-grade stock cabinets with upgrades and a range of standard modifications.

Key to the versatility of these systems is that heights, widths, and depths can be adjusted so they will fit practically any situation.

## Judging Quality

To determine a cabinet's quality, look closely at how it's made. As you compare products from several lines, you'll begin to notice differences.

Start by inspecting the drawers— they take more of a beating than any other part and are a good indication of quality. Slides, critical to the smooth operation of drawers, should be adjustable; determine whether they allow full or only partial extension of the drawers. Also check that drawers align properly when closed and that the

*Custom closet storage includes drawers, hanging racks, shelves, and cubby holes specifically designed to the homeowner's needs.*

DESIGNER: BRENDA LYNE

joinery is well crafted. (For details on drawers, see page 84.)

Then look at the hinges to see if they can be fine-tuned with the cabinets in place. Examine the cabinet doors to see how well they align.

Cabinet boxes (called carcasses) made of plywood are considered to be slightly better than particleboard-base carcasses. Quality cabinets have hardwood plywood or melamine interiors; on lower-quality models, the interior may be raw particleboard or surfaced with vinyl paper. Shelves of ¾-inch plywood are much stronger and less likely to sag than shelves of thinner plywood or particleboard.

## Figuring Costs & Ordering

The range of styles—and prices— makes buying cabinets much like buying a car. Like car makers, every manufacturer picks a market position and

then offers various styles and options that increase or decrease the basic price. If you're looking for the cabinet equivalent of "transportation," you can pay a lot less than someone looking for something sportier.

Know your budget. You'll quickly learn what kinds of cabinets you can afford. With your plan in hand, you can get a base price for standard cabinets relatively easily. But options will drastically alter the quote, so the same basic cabinet can end up costing a lot of different prices. Bids should be full quotes based on a specified sketch listing the options desired in each cabinet.

Remember that, within each line, basic costs are determined by the style of the doors and drawers, as well as by the species of wood used. The basic carcass will be the same no matter what door or drawer style you choose.

Ask for complete shop drawings to avoid any misunderstandings.

# INSTALLING CABINETS

If you have a moderate level of woodworking experience, you can probably install manufactured cabinets (such as those used in a kitchen) yourself. The following information, which assumes a familiarity with common terminology and techniques, outlines the basic steps.

**Wall-mounted cabinets.** To begin, locate the wall studs (see page 71) in the area of your new cabinets and snap chalklines to mark the studs' centers. Next, lay out the cabinets' top line, measuring from the floor in several places (84 inches is common). Use the highest mark for your reference point. Trace a line from this mark across the wall, using a carpenter's level as a straightedge.

Then measure down the exact height of the cabinets from the top line and mark this line on the wall. Temporarily tack a ledger strip to the wall studs, aligning the top of the ledger with the bottom line on the wall.

With a helper or two, lift a cabinet into place atop the ledger. Drill pilot holes through the cabinet's nail rail into studs and loosely fasten the cabinet with 3-inch woodscrews or drywall screws and finishing washers.

Carefully check the cabinet for level and plumb from side to side and front to back. Because walls are seldom exactly plumb, you may have to make some adjustments so the cabinet will hang correctly (bumps or high spots can sometimes be sanded, and low spots can be shimmed).

If your cabinet includes scribing strips along the sides, you can shave them down to achieve a tight fit with an adjoining wall. To scribe a cabinet, run masking tape down the side to be scribed. Setting the points of a compass with pencil to the widest gap between the scribing strip and wall, run the compass down the wall, as shown below, at left. The wall's irregularities will be transferred to the tape. Remove the cabinet from the wall and trim the scribing strip to the line with a plane or belt sander.

When all is in order, tightly screw the cabinet to the wall and recheck with the level.

**Base or floor cabinets.** Remove any baseboard, moldings, or vinyl wall base that might interfere with the placement of the cabinets; then locate studs in the area (if not already done) and mark them as described at left.

If your cabinets have a separate toekick pedestal, set it in place. Once it's shimmed level all around, screw it to studs; then, if necessary, add mitered lumber or plywood facing strips (shown below, at center).

Measure up the exact cabinet height off the floor in several spots; use the highest mark for your reference point. Draw a level line through the mark and across the wall.

If you need to cut an access hole in a cabinet's back or bottom for plumbing lines or electrical boxes, do so now. Then, with helpers, move the cabinet into position. Check level and plumb from side to side and front to back; shim the cabinet, as necessary, between the cabinet base and the floor. If your cabinet includes scribing strips, trim them as described for wall cabinets.

When the cabinet is aligned, drill pilot holes through the nail rail or case back into the studs. Fasten the cabinet to the wall studs with 3-inch woodscrews or drywall screws and finishing washers.

To join adjacent cabinets, clamp them together with C-clamps to align the front edges and screw together adjacent cabinet sides or face frames as shown below, at right.

## Installing Cabinets: Three Tips

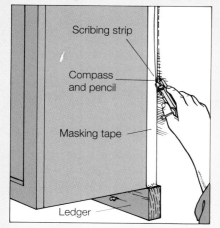

*Use a compass to mark scribing strip when fitting to an irregular wall.*

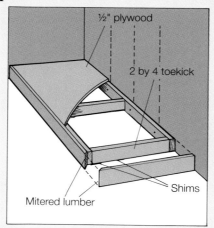

*Shim toekick level, screw to studs, and finish with mitered lumber.*

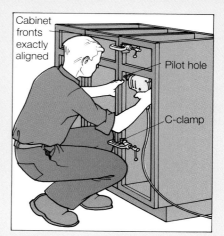

*Clamp cabinets so they're flush; screw adjacent sides or face frames.*

# Shelves

Of all storage and display components, shelves are the most basic. They're installed in cabinets, built into all types of wall units, and simply mounted by themselves on brackets or supports. Some are fixed in place; others are adjustable; still others pull out, swivel, or lift up.

When you start to shop, you'll discover shelves made of a variety of materials, including several kinds of solid wood, laminate- and veneer-covered plywood or particleboard, and glass. When you're building a custom system or designing one with modular components, it pays to know what types of shelves are available so you can specify the ones that best fit the task at hand.

*A sampling of shelf materials features, at left, ⁵⁄₄ by 12 solid oak, 1 by 12 Clear pine, and 2 by 12 Clear fir; at right, ³⁄₈- by 10-inch glass, white oak veneer on a particleboard core, and almond laminate on a particleboard core.*

Before you order, be sure you have a good idea of what you're planning to store on the shelves. That way, you can choose the appropriate material and determine the right span between supports.

## Shelf Materials

How do you choose the right material for your shelving needs? That depends on the appearance and strength you want the shelving to have. Strength is based on the load the shelf will hold and the distance it will span between supports.

Some materials can span farther than others without bowing or breaking under a given load; guidelines are given in the chart on the facing page. Use the maximum spans for lightweight to medium-weight loads, such as art objects, books, pictures, and relatively lightweight electronic gear. For heavier loads, such as televisions, wine racks, or heavy electronic components, shorten the spans or use stronger materials. Place only lightweight objects on glass shelving.

**Pine, fir, and other softwoods.** Sold as boards through lumber dealers, these softwoods are favored for relatively inexpensive, do-it-yourself shelving.

Several grades are available. For most shelving, the appearance grades of Select (sometimes called Clear) and Common are preferred. Look for C-and-better Selects if you want flawless, knotless wood. Other less-expensive choices for shelving are No. 2 and No. 3 Common "knotty" pine. Whatever the grade, let your eyes be the final judge. If your boards require finishing, see page 88 for information.

**Solid hardwoods.** Hardwoods such as oak, birch, and maple are available through hardwood lumber dealers. Hardwoods tend to be quite expensive, particularly in the rare, wide boards required for shelving (for custom shelving, several widths are

sometimes glued together by a cabinetmaker to form a wider board).

**Hardwood-veneered plywood.** Hardwood-veneered plywood is more commonly used for shelving than solid hardwood. Plywood is considerably less expensive, comes in wide (4- by 8-foot) sheets, and won't warp or twist as readily as solid wood. In cabinet construction, the plywood is usually edged with hardwood veneer tape or trimmed with solid hardwood.

**Laminate and melamine.** Popular in European-style wall systems, shelves covered with laminate, melamine, or related films are easy to maintain and relatively inexpensive. Shelves with a core of plywood are a bit sturdier and less likely to sag than those with a core of particleboard or related medium-density fiberboard (MDF).

Of the three surfacing materials, plastic laminate is by far the most durable. Melamine, a surface layer of resin-impregnated paper, is very serviceable and considerably less expensive than plastic laminate. Vinyl paper-wrapped shelves (or shelves made of raw particleboard) are the lowest grade.

**Glass.** Plate glass with ground edges is a popular shelf material for displays because it allows you to view objects more fully and doesn't block the light. Choose ¼-, ⅜-, or ½-inch thicknesses, depending on the span.

## Specialty Shelving

Installing specialty shelving in your custom or modular wall unit adds flexibility and convenience. Some examples are shown at right.

Shelves that pull out like shallow drawers are useful for electronic components, such as top-loading VCRs and turntables. A pullout swiveling shelf for a television allows for a greater range of visibility. Some shelves even lift up from inside a base cabinet to support an appliance at a comfortable working height. And sloped racks display and organize periodicals at a good angle for browsing.

## Specialty Shelves

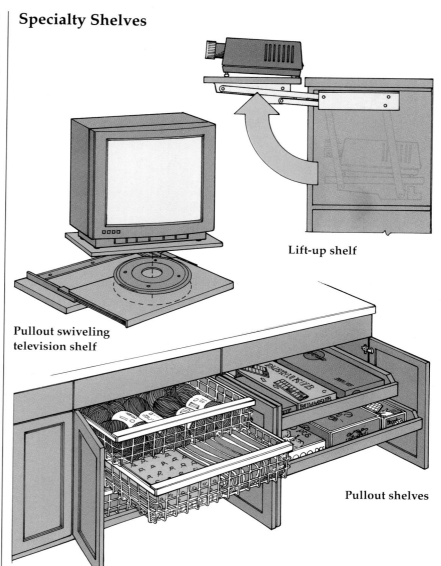

Lift-up shelf

Pullout swiveling television shelf

Pullout shelves

*Special-purpose shelving includes a pullout swiveling television shelf, a lift-up shelf to raise equipment from a base cabinet to comfortable working height, and pullout shelves and baskets handy for low cabinets.*

### MAXIMUM SPANS BETWEEN SUPPORTS

Note: Reduce all spans for heavy loads. Glass shelves are sized for lightweight loads only.

| MATERIAL | SPAN |
|---|---|
| 1-by (¾-inch) pine or fir | 30 inches |
| 2-by (1½-inch) pine or fir | 48 inches |
| 5/4 hardwood | 48 inches |
| ¾-inch plywood-core veneer or laminate | 36 inches |
| ¾-inch particleboard-core veneer or laminate | 24 inches |
| ¼-inch plate glass (12 inches deep) | 36 inches |
| ⅜-inch plate glass (12 inches deep) | 48 inches |
| ½-inch plate glass (12 inches deep) | 60 inches |

# MOUNTING & CUSTOMIZING TRACKS & BRACKETS

## Three Ways to Conceal Shelf Supports

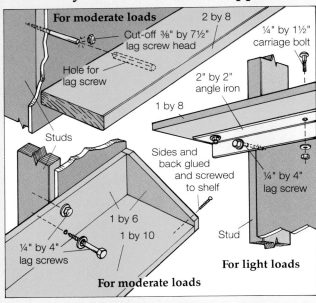

*Where you don't want shelf supports to show, try one of the three shelf-mounting methods shown here.*

**M**ounting shelves on walls is the easiest and least expensive way to provide storage and display space. And because they're adjustable, easy to install, and widely available, tracks and brackets are one of the most popular ways to mount shelves. Where appearance counts, tracks can be customized in a number of ways, as illustrated on the facing page. You can also find mounts that are completely inconspicuous, such as those shown at left.

Brackets are available in several styles and finishes. The most common are sized for 8-, 10-, or 12-inch-wide board shelves. Tracks come in 1- to 4-foot lengths.

## Mounting Tracks & Brackets

Because tracks need to be fastened to studs, which are usually 16 inches apart, your tracks will be 16, 32, or 48 inches apart, depending on your design and the load the shelves will bear. Attach the tracks with screws that penetrate the wood for at least two-thirds their length. (For masonry, use special fasteners, as explained on page 71.)

Locate the studs (see page 71) in the area where you want to place the shelving. If you need to cut tracks to

## How to Mount Tracks & Brackets

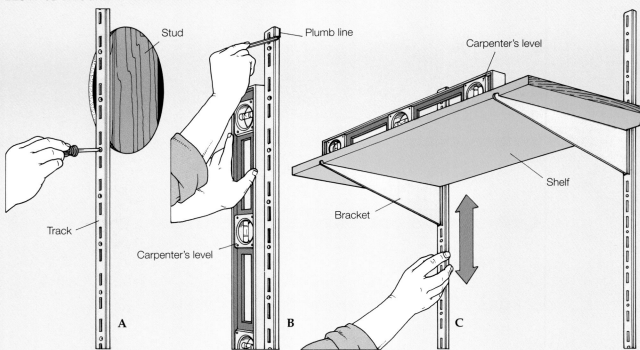

*Drive a screw through track into stud (A); draw a plumb line (B), align track, and fasten. When shelf is level and second track is plumb (C), attach track.*

length, use a hacksaw; just be sure the slots are perfectly aligned from piece to piece.

Place the first track in position over a stud, drill a small pilot hole through one screw hole, and drive in a screw, as shown at the bottom of the facing page; leave the screw slightly loose so you can move the track. Next, check for plumb with a carpenter's level and mark along the track's edge for reference. Align the track with your marks and drill the remaining pilot holes. Then install and tighten all the screws.

Insert a bracket in the first track; then place a bracket in the matching slot of another track. Lift the second track into position, place a shelf across the brackets—you may need a helper for this—and put a level on the shelf as shown on the facing page. Level the shelf by moving the track; then mark the track's top and bottom on the wall. Install the second track as you did the first. Add any other tracks in the same manner.

Finally, install the brackets, locking them into place with a slight downward pull; if they don't seat, lightly tap them down with a hammer.

## Dressing Up Shelf Hardware

Perhaps you'd like a warmer, more custom look than bare shelf hardware provides. Or maybe you prefer not to have the metal tracks show. Here are several ways to combine the efficiency of standard hardware with the character of custom units. (For an illustration of these methods, see at right.)

**Making brackets less noticeable.** To partially hide standard brackets, you can recess their tips. Pick the next smallest bracket than the "right" size for your shelf width and drill ¼-inch-diameter holes where bracket tips will meet shelf bottoms. To take the process one step further, add overhanging lips to shelf fronts.

If you're installing glass shelves, cut off the tips entirely and glue a small rubber or felt pad to the glass.

**Customizing tracks.** Grooved uprights mounted to the wall dress up tracks and brackets. Cut 1 by 2s, 2 by 2s, or similar lumber to track length; then cut grooves to inset the tracks flush with the surface of each upright (you'll need a router or table saw).

You can also install the uprights and tracks away from the wall, facing the brackets inward. This hides the tracks completely—you see only solid wood. Pressure devices or L-brackets hold the uprights in position between the ceiling and floor.

No power tools? Rather than insetting tracks, hide them between adjoining wood strips. Choose molding, trim, or lath that's about the same thickness as the tracks.

## Customizing Shelf Hardware

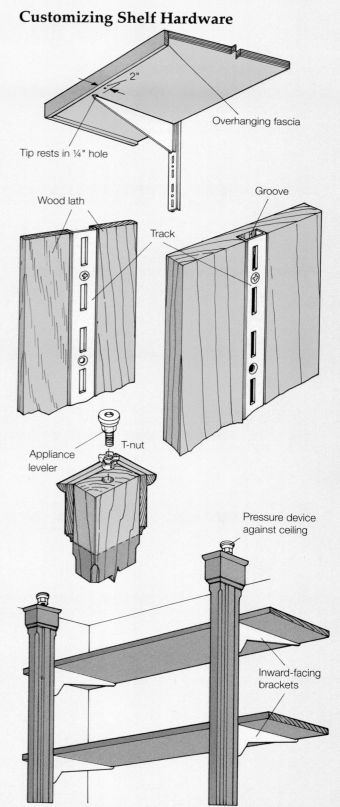

*Shown are several ways to give track-and-bracket hardware a custom look.*

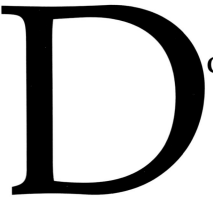

# DOORS FOR CABINETS

Doors hide clutter, seal out dust, and enhance the appearance of cabinets. Whether you're shopping for a modular wall unit or creating custom cabinetry, you'll discover doors come in a variety of styles and materials and can perform different functions.

Cabinet doors can hinge, slide, drop down, fold, or retract. The type that works best on a particular cabinet depends on the purpose.

**Hinged doors**, by far the most common, open easily and allow total access to a cabinet's contents.

**Sliding doors** always look tidy and don't require room to swing, but they allow access only into half the cabinet at a time.

**Drop-down doors**, which swing down rather than to the side, can double as work surfaces when they're placed at the right height.

**Folding and tambour (rollaway) doors** open the cabinet completely; they require little or no swinging room, but they're somewhat awkward to operate.

**Retractable doors** hinge open and then slide back into a cabinet. These doors are particularly effective for television cabinets or where hinged doors would be an obstruction.

*Just a few of the many cabinet doors available include (clockwise from top left) flat laminate door, raised panel door made of stained alder wood, maple frame-and-panel door, plain glass door, flat wood-veneered door, and framed decorative glass door.*

## How Doors Are Made

Cabinet doors are constructed either as flat panels or as a panel surrounded by a frame. The flat-panel type is normally wood veneer or laminate over a core of plywood, particleboard, or medium-density fiberboard (MDF). A frame-and-panel door may be made of solid hardwood or a combination of hardwood and veneered panels.

Glass doors, especially those made of etched, beveled, or leaded glass, may utilize a hardwood frame, much like a frame-and-panel door (the glass replaces the panel). Or glass sheets with ground edges can be fitted into tracks to serve as sliders. Still other glass doors are hinged; some hinges clamp in place on the glass, while others are secured through holes bored in the glass.

Study cabinet doors and you'll notice that there are several ways to mount a door with respect to the cabinet face. A *flush* door is mounted inside the opening, with its face flush with the front of the cabinet or face frame. On a *lipped* door, a rabbet is cut around the inside edges of the door so half its thickness projects beyond the face frame. An *overlay* door overlaps the edges of the opening and is mounted with its inside face against the face frame.

Lipped doors are much more forgiving of slight discrepancies in adjustment than flush and overlay doors.

## Hinges

Shown at right is a sampling of the array of hinges available to hang different types of doors.

European-style hinges, which are hidden behind the door, are by far the most popular for frameless cabinets and modular wall systems. Offset hinges are the standard for face-frame cabinets with lipped doors. The best of these are adjustable and allow a door to open completely—170°—rather than restricting it to a 95° swing.

For particularly heavy or large doors, choose heavy-duty hinges.

DESIGN: EURODESIGN, LTD.　　　DESIGN: EURODESIGN, LTD.

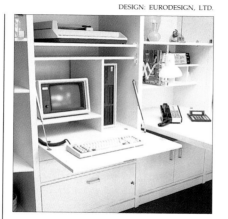 

*Drop-down door (left), fitted with supports, becomes a convenient desk surface. A retractable door, such as the one shown at right, is ideal where an open cabinet door would obstruct movement; this one swings up and slides into the cabinet.*

## Hinges for Cabinet Doors

### Semiconcealed hinges

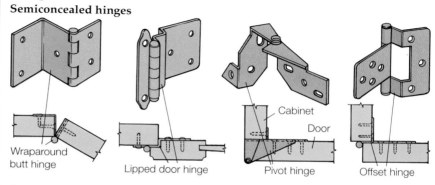

Wraparound butt hinge

Lipped door hinge

Cabinet

Door

Pivot hinge

Offset hinge

### Concealed hinges

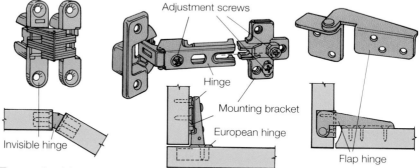

Invisible hinge

Adjustment screws

Hinge

Mounting bracket

European hinge

Flap hinge

### Decorative hinge

### Glass-door hinges

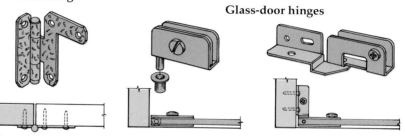

*Hinges are available in a wide variety of looks, from decorative to semiconcealed to completely hidden.*

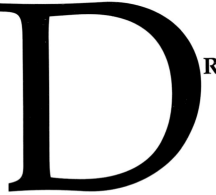

# DRAWERS

Drawers expand a cabinet's storage capacity by allowing accessible storage from front to back. Closed, drawers keep contents protected and out of view; when open, they offer easy access to everything inside.

Drawers are, however, a more expensive form of storage than open shelves or cabinets with doors. For this reason, they're generally specified only where important. Also, because you look into a drawer from above, they're installed mainly in low cabinets; when used in tall units, they're placed no higher than about 50 inches.

## Drawer Construction

A drawer is essentially a box with four sides and a bottom. The manner in which the box is built for a particular cabinet system is a good way to judge the overall quality of the system. The best drawers have hardwood sides dovetailed to a front panel that is separate from the drawer's face (see below). A sturdy ¼-inch hardwood plywood bottom is set into dadoes, or grooves, in the sides, back, and front.

Medium-grade drawers may have sides built of hardwood, seven- or

*When buying drawers, look closely at how they're constructed: from the top, a high-quality hardwood drawer with dovetailed joints; a low-grade, vinyl-wrapped particleboard drawer; and two medium-grade drawers, one made of multilaminated plywood rabbeted to a hardwood front and the other made of a melamine box with a separate front.*

nine-ply hardwood plywood, or melamine-surfaced plywood. Sides may be doweled and glued or rabbeted and screwed to front panels. It's important that they be connected to the front with strong joinery.

Other medium-grade drawers are molded completely from rigid plastics and given a front panel that matches the cabinet system. These drawers are sturdy and maintenance-free.

Lowest-quality drawers are built of particleboard coated with vinyl paper. Some are "folded" together from a single piece and mitered at the corners. Sides are attached directly to the finish front with hot-melt glue and staples, an unreliable method that may result in the drawer's falling apart with time. The bottom is often made of thin, 3/16-inch hardboard.

## Drawer Slides

Though a narrow drawer may be mounted on a center slide, side slides handle more weight and operate more smoothly.

White, epoxy-coated steel slides with nylon rollers are industry standards (see illustration at right). When rollers are rimmed with a rubber ring, operation will be the quietest and smoothest. Though you can get ball-bearing slides, they're unnecessary for all but the heaviest drawers.

Center slides are appropriate only for lightweight, narrow drawers.

The distance that slides extend is important to consider, particularly if you'll be storing items in the backs of drawers. Most drawer slides extend only three-quarters of their length; high-quality slides extend completely. When you close a drawer, high-quality slides will automatically seat the drawer firmly against the cabinet.

*Heavy-duty file drawer offers a double row of storage for hanging files in an office cabinet. This system has file drawers in two or three different widths.*

## Drawer Slide Options

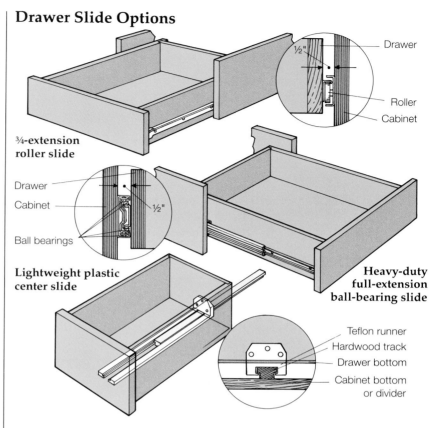

¾-extension roller slide

Lightweight plastic center slide

Heavy-duty full-extension ball-bearing slide

DESIGN: EURODESIGN, LTD.

# SPECIAL COMPONENTS & ACCESSORIES

Nearly all wall system manufacturers offer a few special components and accessories that stretch the capabilities of their cabinetry. Some offer such an extensive range of choices, from beds and desks to organizers and racks, that you can turn an ordinary wall system into a highly organized, multifunctional "machine."

For example, what appears to be a waist-high drawer may be a drop-down door that reveals a pullout ironing board. Deep drawer fronts can hide roomy hanging file systems. A breakfast table or desktop can pull straight out of a wall system or fold down into place. A television can magically rise out of the top of a cabinet.

Most of the hardware for these specialized pieces is produced by specialty hardware manufacturers—mostly European. These products are sold through catalogs to cabinet manufacturers, custom woodworking shops, and some builders' hardware retailers.

When you buy a factory-made wall system, you'll discover some special components and accessories offered as standard options. If you're commissioning cabinets from a custom shop, you can ask to browse through their catalogs to explore the possibilities. Nearly all will be happy to order specialty fixtures and incorporate them into your cabinetry.

DESIGN: EURODESIGN, LTD.

*Specialized accessories make wall systems even more functional. A swing-up shelf (above) raises a typewriter to working height; a keyboard shelf pushes under the counter. A long table (small photo at top) folds out of a cabinet.*

DESIGN: CATHY MOOREHEAD & ASSOCIATES

DESIGN: EURODESIGN, LTD.

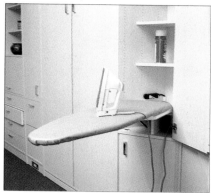

*Disappearing acts include a television lift that electrically raises and lowers the television through the top of a cabinet (left) and an ironing board that folds away into a utility cabinet (above).*

*When a wall system is fitted with a fold-down bed, such as the unit shown above and at right, a home office, a sewing room, or nearly any other area can do double duty as a guest bedroom.*

DESIGN: EURODESIGN, LTD.

# FINISHES FOR FURNITURE

The finish that's applied to wood dramatically affects its appearance. But finishes do more than this—a good finish keeps dirt and moisture out of wood pores, wards off dents, and protects the wood from abrasion, heat, and chemicals.

Solid wood or wood-veneered wall systems can be finished with any of several types of stains, paints, and other coatings (vinyl, melamine, and laminate are actually surface materials, not finishes). The chart on the facing page outlines the characteristics of common wood-finishing products. For additional help, consult your paint dealer.

Finishes are applied in different ways. Some are simply spread onto the wood, leaving the furniture ready for use in a few hours. Others must be applied in several coats and demand much rubbing between coats. Don't just automatically choose the easiest method; you get what you pay for, in time and effort as well as in quality of materials.

**Stains.** Though many woods, especially dark, highly figured species, have beautiful natural color that requires no stain at all, light-colored, nondescript wood can often benefit from the application of a stain. Stains can add color and a bit of character; they can also highlight the grain. They can make one wood species resemble another or blend new and old materials.

In most cases, stains are not final finishes; they're for color or accent only. You still need to seal the surface with a clear finish. If your pieces are made of unfinished pine, seal the wood before staining to achieve even coloring.

Though you may encounter many stain names and brands, products fall into two general types: pigmented stains and dyes.

*Pigmented stains,* sold as oil stain, wood stain, and pigmented wiping stain, are composed of finely ground particles of color held in suspension in oil solvent. Essentially a thin paint, this type of stain lodges in pores and other spaces between wood fibers and tends to conceal the grain. Available in most retail outlets, these stains go on easily with a brush or rag.

*Dyes* are mostly aniline (a coal-tar derivative), dissolved in various substances. Because they're actually absorbed by the wood fibers, they allow the grain to show through. In addition to wood tone, you'll find brilliant colors—wine red, blue, yellow, even bright green. If you can't find dyes at retail stores, look for them at wood-finishing specialty stores.

**Clear finishes.** All clear finishing products generally fall into two basic types: penetrating finishes and surface coatings. Other wood finishes are often variations of these.

*Penetrating finishes* soak into the pores of the wood to give it a natural look and feel. Though a penetrating finish sinks below the wood's surface, it's still fairly durable and can often resist stains, chemicals, and liquids without the "dipped-in-plastic" look of some of the more protective coatings, such as polyurethane.

Natural and synthetic oils and resins are the most popular penetrating finishes. The natural ones have played a major role in furniture finishing for years. Today, however, penetrating resins and rub-on varnishes are more popular because they are as beautiful as natural oil but easier to use.

*Surface coatings* lie on top of the wood and provide protection in the form of a thin, durable shield. This kind of coating, often available in a number of sheens, is glasslike in appearance but can be dulled down, if desired, in a variety of ways. When properly maintained, a good surface finish will protect your storage furniture from dropped objects, scratches, stains, chemicals, heat, and other potential damagers.

*Shellac* is the classic natural surface finish. It's warm toned and subtle, easy to apply, and quick drying. Unfortunately, its alcohol content makes it vulnerable to chemicals, such as a spilled cocktail or detergent.

*Lacquer* is similar to shellac, but it's harder and more durable. It can be rubbed to a high sheen. Because of the beautiful, glossy finish it creates, lacquer is a very popular finish. It's difficult to apply lacquer successfully without spray equipment, though special brushing lacquers are available.

Even though lacquered pieces are beautiful, you may want to rule them out for use in areas where they can get scratched.

*Varnish,* particularly the newer water-base type, is an excellent choice for a durable surface finish. Most modern synthetic finishes, as well as plastic finishes and polyurethanes, are elaborations of varnish's original linseed oil/shellac formulation. On factory-finished pieces, sprayed-on polyurethanes give much the same look as lacquers but are considerably more durable.

**Enamel paints.** Water-base (latex) and oil-base (alkyd) enamels are often used for interior surfaces. Latex paints are easier to use because water is their solvent, but alkyds are more durable.

Paint finishes range from flat, or matte, to high gloss. Since there's no industry standard for sheens, a medium gloss may be called pearl, semigloss, or some other name, and it can range from moderately to very shiny, depending on the manufacturer. The glossier the finish, the more durable and washable it is.

# A LOOK AT FINISHING PRODUCTS

## STAINS

| | |
|---|---|
| **Pigmented oil stain** | Simple to apply; won't fade or bleed. Useful for making one wood species look like another. Heavy pigments tend to obscure grain and gum up pores in such hardwoods as oak and walnut. Not compatible with shellac or lacquer. |
| **Penetrating oil stain** | One-step product stains with dyes rather than pigments, so pores and grain show through. Similar to penetrating resin, but with color added. Produces irregular results on softwoods and plywoods. Handy for repairs, touch-up jobs. |
| **Gel stain** | May contain both pigments and dyes. Very easy to apply (just wipe on and let dry), but results may be uneven on large surfaces. |
| **Aniline dye** (water base) | Colors are brilliant, clear, and permanent. Since water raises wood grain, resanding is necessary. Very slow drying. Sold in powdered form; may be hard to find. |
| **Aniline dye** (alcohol base) | Quick-drying alcohol stains won't raise grain, but they aren't very light-fast; best reserved for small touch-up jobs. Should be sprayed on to avoid lap marks. |
| **Non-grain-raising stain** | Bright, transparent colors; won't raise wood grain. Available premixed by mail. Very short drying time; best when sprayed. Not for use on softwoods. |

## PENETRATING FINISHES

| | |
|---|---|
| **Boiled linseed oil** | Lends warm, slightly dull patina to wood. Dries very slowly and requires many coats. Moderate resistance to heat, water, and chemicals. Easily renewable. |
| **Tung oil** | Natural oil finish that's hard and highly resistant to abrasion, moisture, heat, acid, and mildew. Requires several thin, hand-rubbed applications (heavy coats wrinkle badly). Best with polymer resins added. |
| **Penetrating resin** (Danish oil, antique oil) | Use on hard, open-grain woods. Leaves wood looking and feeling "natural." Easy to apply and retouch, but doesn't protect against heat or abrasion. May darken some woods. |
| **Rub-on varnish** | Penetrating resin and varnish combination that builds up sheen as coats are applied; dries fairly quickly. Moderately resistant to water and alcohol. Darkens wood. |

## SURFACE FINISHES

| | |
|---|---|
| **Shellac** | Lends warm luster to wood. Easy to apply, retouch, and remove. Excellent sealer. Lays down in thin, quick-drying coats that can be rubbed to a high sheen. Little resistance to heat, alcohol, and moisture. Comes in white (blonde), orange, and brownish (button) versions. Available in flake form or premixed. |
| **Lacquer** (nitrocellulose) | Strong, clear, quick-drying finish in both spraying and brushing form. Very durable, though vulnerable to moisture. Requires 3 or more coats; can be polished to a high gloss. Noxious fumes; highly flammable. |
| **Lacquer** (water base) | Easier to clean, less toxic, and much less flammable than nitrocellulose lacquer—more practical spray product for do-it-yourselfer. Raises grain; use sanding sealer. May dry more slowly than nitrocellulose lacquer. Can smell strongly of ammonia. |
| **Varnish** (oil base) | Widely compatible oil-base interior varnish that produces a thick coating with good overall resistance. Dries slowly and darkens with time. Brush marks and dust can be a problem. |
| **Varnish** (water base) | Easy cleanup. Dries quickly; nontoxic when dry. Though early versions lacked durability, new products are greatly improved. Finish goes on milky, but dries clear and won't yellow. Raises wood grain. May require numerous coats. Expensive. |
| **Polyurethane varnish** | Thick, plastic, irreversible coating that's nearly impervious to water, heat, and alcohol. Dries overnight. Incompatible with some stains and sealers. Follow instructions to ensure good bonding between coats. |
| **Enamel** | Available in flat, semigloss, and gloss finishes, and in a wide range of colors. May have lacquer or varnish (alkyd, water, or polyurethane) base; each shares same qualities as clear finish of the same type. |
| **Wax** | Occasionally used as a finish, especially on antiques or "aged" pine. More often applied over harder top coats. Increases luster of wood. Not very durable, but offers some protection against liquids when renewed frequently. Available in various shades. |

# LIGHTING

Whether you use wall systems to conceal clutter or to display treasures, you must pay attention to one essential ingredient: light. Light, both natural and artificial, helps you find and identify items on shelves, in cabinets, and in drawers, and can highlight artwork and collections worth seeing. With the proper lighting, your wall system becomes not only more functional but also more aesthetically pleasing.

Of course, natural light is critical to the success of any room. Before deciding where to place a storage unit, consider how you can make best use of natural light. A source of daylight across from your unit will bathe your shelving in a soft, glare-free glow; closer by, it can accent a particular grouping or display. In any room being used as a home theater, be sure to provide a way to shut out natural light when it's unwanted.

## Lighting Basics

Today's designers separate lighting into three categories: task, accent, and ambient. All three can be used for lighting wall systems.

*Mounted inside the door frame of this antique Welsh cupboard (shown left), strip lighting illuminates a collection of porcelains and Staffordshire dogs. Mini light strips (shown above), with self-adhesive backing, are easy to install.*

***Task lighting.*** Task lighting does just what it says—it illuminates a particular area where a visual activity, such as reading, writing, or sewing, takes place. It's often achieved with individual fixtures that direct light onto the work surface.

***Accent lighting.*** Primarily decorative, accent lighting is used to focus attention on artwork, to highlight architectural features, to set a mood, and to provide drama. It's similar to task lighting in that it consists largely of directional light.

***Ambient, or general, lighting.*** Ambient lighting fills in undefined areas with a soft level of light—say, enough to watch television by or to navigate safely through a room. Ambient lighting usually comes from indirect fixtures that provide a diffuse spread of illumination.

This type of light is best for collections of books and tapes or for glare-free illumination of a display. Directional fixtures can also be aimed at a wall to provide a wash of soft light.

## Light Fixtures

A variety of fixtures is used in and around wall systems to provide all types of lighting. If you're building a custom unit, consider adding recessed

*In this combination dining room/library, bookshelves and display niches are softly lit. Recessed downlights wash artwork, while little lamps tucked into the shelves add a special glow.*

ARCHITECT: TOM WILSON
INTERIOR DESIGNER: KAREN GRAUL

DESIGN: CALVIN L. SMITH ASSOCIATES, LTD.

*Minimal and strikingly contemporary low-voltage light fixtures mount directly on floor-to-ceiling cables. They're easily adjusted to spot objects on display. (For another look at this wall system, turn to page 22.)*

or indirect lighting during construction. Installing such lighting may require the services of an electrician.

**Movable fixtures.** Table lamps, floor lamps, and specialty lamps are easy to buy, easy to change, and easy to take along when you move. They can provide task, accent, or ambient lighting.

Adjustable task lamps and clip-on lights supply a small, bright pool of light while leaving your work area uncluttered. Minireflector spotlights on the floor or on a nearby shelf are handy for highlighting art. Halogen lamps produce the cleanest, tightest beam. Fluorescent models are best for reducing glare and shadows.

## A Selection of Light Fixtures

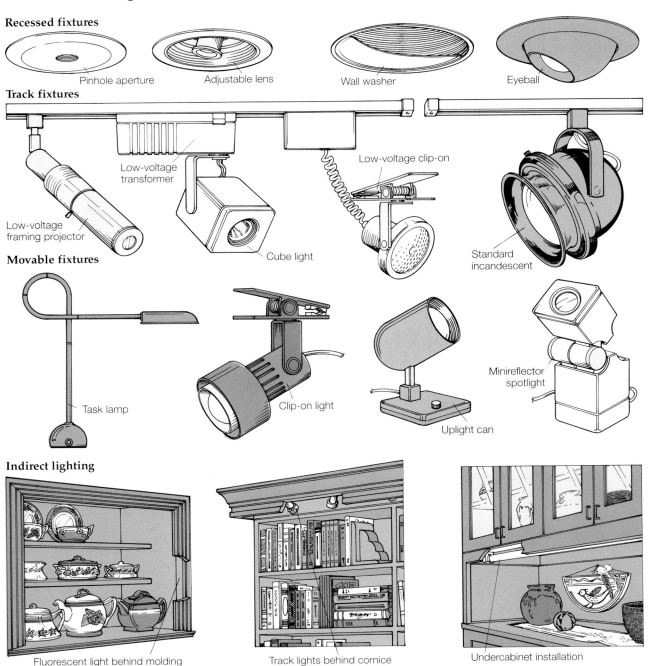

**Recessed fixtures**

Pinhole aperture

Adjustable lens

Wall washer

Eyeball

**Track fixtures**

Low-voltage transformer

Low-voltage clip-on

Low-voltage framing projector

Cube light

Standard incandescent

**Movable fixtures**

Task lamp

Clip-on light

Minireflector spotlight

Uplight can

**Indirect lighting**

Fluorescent light behind molding

Track lights behind cornice

Undercabinet installation

**Track lighting.** Track lighting offers great versatility and ease of installation. Tracks can be suspended from ceilings or mounted flush on walls or ceilings. They can use a large selection of standard incandescent lights, as well as low-voltage fixtures. Some low-voltage fixtures have an integral transformer; others fit a standard track with an adapter. Other tracks require an external transformer mounted away from the track.

Accessories for track fixtures include filters, baffles, and louvers; all allow for greater light control. Framing projectors, which throw a controlled light beam, and minitracks (scaled-down systems for shelves) are especially effective for spotlighting artwork on a wall or shelf.

**Recessed fixtures.** Recessed downlights offer light without the intrusion of a visible fixture. Low-voltage downlights, especially those with MR-16 bulbs and black baffles, are very popular for accent lighting. Like their track counterparts, many low-voltage downlights include an integral transformer; you can also use one external transformer to serve several fixtures.

Equipped as a wall-washer fixture, a recessed downlight throws light onto a nearby wall; a series of such fixtures can be used for even, balanced lighting of a wall unit.

Recessed lights can also be built into light boxes above or below a set of shelves (glass shelves enhance the play of light in such installations).

**Built-in indirect lighting.** Shelving bays, coves, and soffits can be used when indirect, or concealed, lighting is desired. Indirect lighting installed in shelf bays can highlight artwork and provide ambient light. Coves direct light upward onto the ceiling. Soffits, used over display or task areas, throw a strong light directly below.

*Track lighting offers the ultimate in flexibility: each fixture can be moved or adjusted to provide light where it's needed.*

*Elegantly simple formed tube holds tiny low-voltage bulbs. This fixture, sold in many standard lengths and available in custom sizes, comes in chrome, black, white, and custom color finishes. Wires run to a remote transformer. (For another view, see page 28.)*

DESIGN: MICHAEL SOUTER OF LUMINAE SOUTER

DESIGN: AMY SCOTT

# INFORMATION SOURCES

Whether you're shopping for wall systems or working with a designer or cabinet-maker to create custom solutions, you'll find a wealth of ideas and information in brochures offered by the manufacturers and associations listed here. They can also direct you to local outlets and distributors. The addresses and phone numbers in this list are accurate as of press time.

The Yellow Pages of your telephone directory can help you locate furniture dealers, home centers, cabinetmakers, designers, architects, and other manufacturers and associations near you.

## CABINETS
**(Manufactured Stock, Custom & Semicustom)**

**Aristokraft, Inc.**
P.O. Box 420
Jasper, IN 47546
812-482-2527

**Fieldstone Cabinetry, Inc.**
Hwy 105 E. P.O. Box 109
Northwood, IA 50459
800-339-5369
fieldstonecabinetry.com

**Haas Cabinet Co., Inc.**
625 W. Utica Street
Sellersburg, IN 47172
800-457-6458

**KraftMaid Cabinetry, Inc.**
16052 Industrial Parkway
Middlefield, OH 44062
800-814-0480
www.kraftmaid.com

**Merillat Industries, Inc.**
P.O. Box 1946
Adrian, MI 49221
517-263-0771

**Quaker Maid Kitchens**
4203 Pottsville Pike #A
Reading, PA 19605
610-921-2045

**Rutt Custom Cabinetry**
1564 Main Street
P.O. Box 129
Goodville, PA 17528
800-706-7888

**Starmark Cabinets**
P.O. Box 84810
Sioux Falls, SD 57118
605-335-8600

**Wood-Mode, Inc.**
One Second Street
Kreamer, PA 17833
570-374-2711

## CABINETS
**(Modular Systems, Ready-to-Assemble & Imported)**

**eurodesign, ltd.**
359 State Street
Los Altos, CA 94024
650-941-7761

**IKEA**
Plymouth Meeting Hall
Plymouth Meeting, PA 19462
800-434-IKEA

**Planum, Inc.**
www.planumfurniture.com

**Poggenpohl U.S., Inc.**
145 U.S. Highway 46 West
Suite 200
Wayne, NJ 07470
973-812-8900

**Roche-Bobois U.S.A. Ltd.**
183 Madison Avenue
New York, NY 10016
212-889-5304

**SieMatic**
Two Greenwood Square
3331 Street Road, Suite 450
Bensalem, PA 19020
215-244-6800

**Techline by Marshall Erdman and Associates, Inc.**
500 South Division Street
Waunakee, WI 53597
800-356-8400

## FURNITURE
**(Storage & Display)**

**Bernhardt Furniture Co.**
1031 Morganton Blvd. SW
Lenoir, NC 28645
828-758-0532

**Conran's Habitat**
800-3-CONRANS

**Drexel Heritage Furnishings, Inc.**
2200 Highway 70, SE
Hickory, NC 28602
828-326-1060
www.drexelheritage.com

**Ethan Allen Inc.**
Ethan Allen Drive
P.O. Box 1966
Danbury, CT 06813-1966
203-743-8000
www.ethanallen.com

**Habersham Plantation**
P.O. Box 1209
Toccoa, GA 30577
800-HABERSHAM

**Henredon Furniture Industries**
P.O. Box 70
Morganton, NC 28680-0070
800-444-3682

**Lexington Furniture Industries**
117 Winchester Road
Lexington, Kentucky 40505
704-249-5300

**Lineage Home Furnishings, Inc.**
P.O. Box 1354
Lexington, NC 27293-1354
336-249-4931

**Thomasville Furniture
Industries, Inc.**
P.O. Box 339
Thomasville, NC 27361
800-225-0265

**Wellington Hall, Ltd.**
P.O. Box 1354
Lexington, NC 27293
800-262-1049

# LIGHTING

**American Lighting
Association**
P.O. Box 420288
Dallas, TX 75342
800-274-4484

**Artemide Litech**
1980 New Highway
Farmingdale, NY 11735
516-694-9292

**Capri Lighting**
6430 E. Slauson Avenue
Los Angeles, CA 90040
213-726-1800

**Cooper Lighting**
400 Busse Road
Elk Grove Village, IL 60007
847-956-8400
www.cooperlighting.com

**CSL Lighting
Manufacturing, Inc.**
14625 E. Clark Avenue
City of Industry, CA 91745
626-336-4511

**FLOS Inc.**
200 McKay Road
Huntington Station, NY
11746
516-549-2745

**George Kovacs Lighting**
67-25 Otto Road
Glendale, NY 11385
718-628-5201

**Juno Lighting, Inc.**
2001 S. Mount Prospect Road
Des Plaines, IL 60017-5065
847-827-9880

**Lightolier/Genlyte**
100 Lighting Way
Secaucus, NJ 07096
800-628-8692

**Reggiani U.S.A.**
P.O. Box 4270
New Windsor, NY 12553
914-565-8500

**Ron Rezek Lighting**
4200 Sepulveda Boulevard
Culver City, CA 90230
310-836-1572

**Tech Lighting**
1718 West Fullerton
Chicago, IL 60614
773-883-6110

**Translite Systems**
1300 Industrial Way #19
San Carlos, CA 94070
800-473-3242

# MOLDINGS &
# MILLWORK

**Executive Woodsmiths, Inc.**
2711 Wilkinson Blvd.
Charlotte, NC 28208
800-951-9090

**Flex Trim Industries**
P.O. Box 4227
Rancho Cucamonga, CA
91730
800-356-9060

**Focal Point Architectural
Products**
3006 Anaconda Drive
Tarboro NC 27886
800-662-5550

**Fypon Molded Millwork**
22 West Pennsylvania Ave.
Stewartstown, PA 17363
800-537-5349

**Like Wood**
12 Arentzen Blvd.
Charleroi, PA 15022
800-367-1076

**Outwater Plastics
Industries, Inc.**
4 Passaic Street
Wood-Ridge, NJ 07075
800-631-8375

**Silverton Victorian
Millworks**
P.O. Box 2987
Durango, CO 81302
800-933-3930

# SHELVING,
# HARDWARE &
# ACCESSORIES

**Closet Maid**
P.O. Box 4400
Ocala, FL 34478
800-874-0008

**Häfele America Co.**
A 3901 Cheyenne Drive
P.O. Box 4000
Archdale, NC 27263
336-889-2322

**Hettich America, L.P.**
6225 Shiloh Road
Alpharette, GA 30005-8348
800-438-8424

**Iron-A-Way Inc.**
220 W. Jackson
Morton, IL 61550
309-266-7232

**Lee/Rowan Company**
900 S. Highway Drive
Fenton, MO 63026
800-325-6150

**Putnam Rolling
Ladder Co., Inc.**
32 Howard Street
New York, NY 10013
212-226-5147

**Rev-A-Shelf, Inc.**
2409 Plantside Drive
P.O. Box 99585
Jefferson, KY 40299
800-626-1126

**Schulte Corporation**
12115 Ellington Court
Cincinnati, OH 45249
800-669-3225

**SICO Room Makers**
P.O. Box 1169
Minneapolis, MN 55440
800-328-6138

# INDEX

Boldface numbers refer to photographs.

Accessories, specialized, 86–87
    information sources, 95
Anchors, for fastening, 71
Architects, 18
Audio equipment. *See*
    Electronic equipment
Audio tapes, 15, 17, **34, 35**

Bathrooms, 13, **49**
Bedrooms, **10,** 13, **25, 42, 43,
    44, 45, 51, 52–53, 56, 74**
Beds, **43, 44, 56**
    fold-down, **52, 87**
Boards, **25**
Bolts, toggle, 71
Books, 14
    typical sizes, 15
    walls, **26–29**
Bookshelves, **1, 4, 5, 9, 10,
    12,** 19, **23, 26, 27, 28, 29,
    39, 40, 46, 54, 55, 56, 57,
    58, 59, 60, 61, 62, 63, 64
    65, 70, 90, 93**
    ideal dimensions, 14
Brackets, **24, 25,** 80–81
Built-ins, 9

Cabinets, **2, 4, 5, 8, 9, 11, 12,
    16, 17, 30, 31, 32–33, 34,
    35, 36, 37, 38, 39, 40, 41,
    42, 43, 44, 45, 46, 47, 48,
    52–53, 54, 55, 56, 58, 60,
    61, 64, 68, 69, 70, 71, 72,
    73, 74, 76, 83, 86, 87**
    for children, **42–45**
    doors for, 82–83
    information sources, 94
    installing, 71, 77
    manufactured, shopping
    for, 74–76
Children's rooms, **13, 25,
    42–45, 51, 56**
China cabinet, **37, 60, 69,** 70
Clear finishes, 88, 89
Closet, **51**
Collectibles, 14
Collection displays, 36–38
Collections, furniture, 69
Color, **2,** 19, **20–21, 40, 41,
    45, 62, 65**
Compact discs, 15, 17, **35**
Components, specialized,
    **86, 87**
    information sources, 94–95
    shopping for, 86–87
Computers, **1, 4, 5, 83, 86**
Concealed lighting, **10, 63, 92**
    built-in, 93
Contractors 19
Cubbyholes, **32, 36, 37, 47,
    49, 50, 54, 59**

Custom cabinets, **74,** 76

Design, and style, 9–10
Designers, 18–19
Desks, **1, 4, 5, 8, 13, 43, 44,
    52–53, 54, 55, 83, 86**
Dining rooms, 12–13, **46, 53,
    54, 72**
Dishes, 13–14
Display, **8, 10, 16, 20–21, 22,
    23, 24, 25, 36, 37, 38,
    39, 40, 44, 45, 46, 47,
    48, 49, 54, 57, 58, 61,
    63, 69, 90, 91**
    art of, 39
Dividers, room, **23, 35, 46–47**
Doors, cabinets, 9, **33, 58, 60,
    64, 69, 76, 82, 83**
    drop-down, **8, 43, 52, 82, 83**
    folding, **5,** 82
    glass, **16, 60,** 70, **73, 82**
    hinged, 82
    retractable, **5, 17, 30, 34, 35,
    73,** 82, **83**
    shopping for, 82–83
    sliding, 82
    tambour, **53,** 82
Drawers, **2, 4, 5, 8, 11, 12, 16,
    17, 20, 34, 35, 42, 43, 44,
    52–53, 54, 55, 69, 72, 74,
    82, 84, 85**
    shopping for, 84–85
Drop-down doors, **8, 43, 52,
    82, 83**

Electronic equipment, **16, 17,
    30, 31, 32, 32, 33, 34, 35,
    43, 49, 52, 54, 64, 69, 70,
    73, 79, 87**
    cabinetry for, 15, 16–17
Enamel paints, 88, 89

Face-frame cabinets, 74
Fasteners, 71
File drawer, **85**
Finishes, for furniture, 88–89
Fireplaces, **12, 40–41**
Fixtures, light. *See* Lighting
Fold-down beds, **52, 87**
Folding doors, **5,** 82
Frameless cabinets, 74–75
Furniture, 8–9
    finishes, 88–89
    information sources, 94
    storage, 68–70

Glass doors, 70, **73, 82**
Glasses, 13–14
Glass shelves, **10, 30, 38, 54,
    61, 78**
    shopping for, 79

Hardware, **5, 11**
    information sources, 95
    shopping for, 83, 86–87
Hinges, 83
Home offices, **5, 52, 54, 55,
    83, 85, 86**

Indirect lighting, **10, 63, 92,** 93
Information sources, 94–95
Installation, of components,
    71, 77
Interior designers, 18
Ironing boards, **55, 87**

Joists, 71

Kitchens, 13, **22, 24, 35, 37,
    38, 47, 50, 55, 61**

Ladders, **4, 10, 23, 28, 29, 48**
    library, 29
Laminate, 11, 79
Laundry areas, 13, **55**
Libraries, **6, 9, 23, 26, 28, 29,
    91, 93**
Library ladders. *See* Ladders
Lift-up shelves, 79, **86, 87**
Lighting, **8, 10,** 27, **28, 35, 36,
    37, 50, 52, 61, 62, 63, 90,
    91, 93**
    information sources, 94–95
    shopping for, 90–93
Lighting designers, 18
Living rooms, 12, **27, 46, 58**
Low-voltage lighting, **8, 28,
    36, 50, 61, 92, 93**

Magazines, 14
Manufactured cabinets
    information sources, 94
    installing, 71, 77
    shopping for, 74–76
Masonry anchors, 71
Materials, 10–11
Media centers. *See* Electronic
    equipment
Media center specialists,
    18–19
Melamine, 79. *See also*
    Laminate
Modular systems, **2, 5 ,8, 11,
    13, 43, 44, 45, 51, 52,
    70, 72, 73, 83, 85, 86, 87**
    information sources, 94
    installing, 71, 77
    shopping for, 72–73
Modules, **45, 53**
Moldings, **12, 31, 33, 62, 65**
    information sources, 95
    magic with, 65
Movable fixtures, 92

Nightstand, 52

Paints, enamel, 88, 89
Partitions, **35, 46–47**
Penetrating finishes, 88, 89
Planning, 7–19
Plywood, for shelves, 79
Professionals 18–19
Pullout shelves, **5, 9, 17, 33,
    34, 54, 73, 79, 83**

Ready-to-assemble (RTA)
    systems, 72–73
    information sources, 94

Recessed lighting, **36, 52, 58,
    61, 91,** 92, 93
Records, 15, 17, **33**
Retail specialists, 18
Retractable doors, **5, 17, 30,
    34, 35, 73, 82, 83**
Room dividers, **23, 35, 46–47**

Semicustom cabinets,
    **66–67,** 76
Shelves, **5, 8, 9, 10, 13, 14,
    15, 17, 20–21, 22, 23,
    24, 25, 30, 33, 34, 35,
    36, 38, 39, 41, 43, 44,
    45, 46, 47, 48, 50, 51,
    52, 53, 54, 55, 56, 57,
    59, 61, 62, 63, 65, 69,
    73, 76, 78, 83, 86, 91**
    dimensions, 14, 15
    information sources, 95
    installing, 71, 80–81
    materials, 78
    shopping for, 78–79
    spans, 79
Shopper's guide, 67–95
Sizing a wall system, 15
Slides, drawer, 85
Spans, shelf, 79
Speakers, **17, 31, 43**
Specialized components and
    accessories, **86, 87**
    information sources, 94–95
    shopping for, 86–87
Spreading anchors, 71
Stains, 88, 89
Stock cabinets, 75–76
Storage furniture, 68–70
Studies, **27, 28**
Studs, 71
Style and design, 9–10
Surface finishes, 88, 89

Tables, **53, 86**
Tambour doors, **50, 53,** 82
Tapes, 15, 17, **34, 35**
Televisions. *See* Electronic
    equipment
Toggle bolts, 71
Track lighting, 92, 93
Tracks and brackets, **25,**
    80–81
Turntables, **33, 34**

Utility areas, 13, **55, 87**

Video equipment. *See*
    Electronic equipment
Videotapes, 15, 17, **34, 35**

Wine storage, **49**
Wood, 10–11
    finishes, 88–89
    for shelves, 78–79
Woodcrafters, 19